PENGUIN BOOKS
THE GLORY IN US ALL

Dr Cassandra Aasmundsen-Fry, Psy.D, is a clinical psychologist with a doctorate in clinical psychology, whose career has been based in Boston, Massachusetts. She has founded MindWell: Modern Psychology and Therapy, a mental health practice in bustling Kuala Lumpur, Malaysia, and is a practising psychologist who works with couples and individuals of all ages.

Dr Aasmundsen-Fry specializes in working with clients who have trauma, complicated families, and relationships and psychological issues that hold them back from having a purpose and feeling content in their lives. She is of mixed race European and Malaysian origin, a dual citizen of the USA and Norway, with experience working with diverse individuals from expats to refugees. She is passionate about equal rights, diversity of thought, race, and culture. Her approach to therapy and writing reflects the belief that we bury the best and worst parts of ourselves but that embracing both allows us to grow and realize our full potential.

The Glory in Us All

Embracing the Life and Knowledge We Bury

Dr Cassandra Aasmundsen-Fry

PENGUIN BOOKS
An imprint of Penguin Random House

PENGUIN BOOKS

Penguin Books is an imprint of the Penguin Random House group of companies whose addresses can be found at global.penguinrandomhouse.com

Published by Penguin Random House SEA Pte Ltd
40 Penjuru Lane, #03-12, Block 2
Singapore 609216

First published in Penguin Books by Penguin Random House SEA 2025

Copyright © Dr Cassandra Aasmundsen-Fry 2025

All rights reserved

10 9 8 7 6 5 4 3 2 1

The views and opinions expressed in this book are the author's own and the facts are as reported by her which have been verified to the extent possible, and the publishers are not in any way liable for the same.

Please note that no part of this book may be used or reproduced in any manner for the purpose of training artificial intelligence technologies or systems.

ISBN 9789815204926

Typeset in Garamond by MAP Systems, Bengaluru, India

This book is sold subject to the condition that it shall not, by way of trade or otherwise, be lent, resold, hired out, or otherwise circulated without the publisher's prior consent in any form of binding or cover other than that in which it is published and without a similar condition including this condition being imposed on the subsequent purchaser.

To my children, I hope you become who you want to be

Contents

Introduction	ix
Preface	xi

Part I: How We Become Who We Are

Chapter 1: Epigenetics	3
Chapter 2: Intergenerational Trauma	19
Chapter 3: Attachment	45

Part II: That Which Shapes Us Along the Way

Chapter 4: Trauma and Psychological Distress	73
Chapter 5: Family Dynamics	109
Chapter 6: Grief and Loss	145

Part III: What We Do Not Know, We Do Not Know

Chapter 7: Defence Mechanisms and Maladaptive Coping	161
Chapter 8: Thought Distortions and Negative Thinking	169
Chapter 9: An Examined Life: Embracing the Life We Bury	179
Acknowledgments	185
Endnotes	187

Introduction

> 'Tell me, what is it you plan to do
> with your one wild and precious life?'
>
> —Mary Oliver

Working with clients for the past fifteen years, I've always been struck by the parts of someone's story yet to be discovered, to be unravelled by reading between the lines and seeing the person in front of me take shape. It is hard to predict who a person is. And it does not always reflect what they choose to reveal. But, over the course of the first few sessions, their fears and struggles become apparent from what they choose to share and perhaps even more so through what lies just outside of their conscious awareness.

Most of us struggle to say who we are. To say it and really own it with certainty and confidence. Sometimes, we have never had a parent look at us with the adoration and protection, reflecting behaviours that are precursors to a healthy sense of self-worth, connection with others, and trust in the world. Other times, we even survive experiences that forever change who we are.

Sometimes, those who believe they know themselves with certainty are the ones who know least about themselves, who possess the least capacity or desire for introspection and self-reflection. These are people who come to therapy and fight to prove to their therapists that they are someone, a particular type of person—generous, moral, kind—or that they belong to some kind of enlightened group, which has figured out the best way to be human. Other times, people seek therapy because they feel like their life is in pieces or they cannot feel happy, but they fight to keep certain illusions—whether these may be their 'ideal' childhood, their partner's love for them being healthy, or them not deserving more—intact.

I understand the desire to feel certain—to feel certain is to feel safe. However, we are all good and bad—a sum of our experiences, connections with others, roads taken and missed, and intergenerational legacies, enriched and limited by culture. And, in the middle of it all, we are full of contradictions and things we do not know about ourselves.

This book aims to explore how we come to be through a series of events and processes existing just outside our consciousness. Fascinatingly and amazingly, we are the products of more forces than we imagine. When people come to me seeking therapy, they are searching for meaning and contentment in their lives because while they may think they know what has shaped them, they cannot feel connected to others or themselves and continue to feel stuck. We are here to discuss all that we bury, since generations past and in our lives at present.

Preface

It is no accident that I have been focused on what we bury and that which is unseen. I have lived my life between the lines of cultures, generations, and the certainty that comes with knowing where you come from. I grew up as the first daughter of a Norwegian father and Malaysian mother. Answering the question where I was from was never simple. I was born in Singapore, and by the time I was nine, I had lived in Sweden, England, and then Saudi Arabia—where I spent some of the most confusing and formative years through high school. I knew next to nothing about the ethnic heritages of my parents. My mother was not just Malaysian but Malaysian Indian; not just Tamil, which the majority of Indian Malaysians are, but Punjabi Indian and Sikh. Our connection to Norway was tenuous. I remember people struggling to put me in a box in college, asking, 'Well, where were you born?' This would lead to a dead end when they would realize Singapore was a mere blip I did not remember. When asked where my parents were from, I could not comment on either of their countries properly or own that heritage because I never lived there. Finally, someone would ask triumphantly, 'Well, where is your passport from?' This would lead to another dead end. As this conversation would usually occur when I first met people, it overwhelmed and shaped how I felt seen. Even to this day, my husband laughs and rolls his eyes when someone asks me where I am from. Try as I might, I've never been able to give a simple answer.

I thought about all these connections or the lack thereof as I became a third culture or expat kid living in Saudi. A third culture kid is someone who has spent most of their lives living in countries other than the cultures of their parents. I completed my middle and high school in Saudi Arabia without any conception of how important home is in grounding your sense of identity—your values, conceptualization of the world, and future self are rooted in the home and the extended family around it. My family was pretty easy-going about religion and spirituality being subjective and people having vastly different ideas of how to live a life—who were we to say what was right or wrong?

Saudi Arabia is a lot to comprehend for a third culture kid. As a foreigner there, you live in compounds—walled in residences of up to 200 houses full of people from all over the world. Your life exists within those walls, even more so if you have been enrolled in a school of your local culture. In my case, I swiftly moved to the American school from the British school, swapping a British accent for an American one as time passed. I did not have any idea what that represented, as I was in no way American (but came to be later in ways as you will find out). Strangely, this switch did not come with a greater sense of belonging. Looking back, I was trying to discover what I did not know, what was between those lines, but did not know where to look.

Living in the bubble of a compound with other third culture kids along with myriad changing identities and struggling with emotional complexities we could not fathom, unsurprisingly, led to more than usual failures in coping and attempts to connect gone wrong (think teenage drinking, inappropriate relationships).

Let's take that confusing foundation and add the single largest predictor of buried feelings and knowledge—trauma. In 2004, the compounds housing foreigners in Saudi Arabia were bombed, followed by a period of instability and threats towards foreigners. Our school shut down, tanks and army units moved into the outskirts of compounds and schools—camouflaged to intruders but like a dagger to our emotions and sense of safety every time we passed them. It was a time of great confusion, fear, and uncertainty. Many of my classmates were affected, many left. The walls between foreigners and locals seemed to harden. No one had the words to explain what was happening, and we did not know what we did not know. We did not process it. What we buried and carried with us was minimized but not forgotten at an unconscious level.

This was when I started feeling the pull towards the field of human behaviour, particularly trauma and identity. I went on to live in the US for a long time. I worked with refugees, clients who had experienced significant abuse and trauma, those figuring out who they were and what they wanted, and everything in between. People could understand their pain—the way their pain thwarted them living a regular life—but had difficulty understanding what stood between them and a life worth living. I was drawn to those who feel broken in a hundred different ways but cannot tolerate saying they had a difficult childhood or that their trauma is not actually their fault. So much of their lives are buried under being the person they think they ought to be, the person a parent expected them to be, or a partner broke them into being.

I learned that I could hear and witness incredible heartbreak, trauma, and strength and offer a safe space in return. I became passionate about firmly hoping that we are a product of our experiences, legacies, and biological narratives. This awareness did not discourage me but was a call to action to examine life to live consciously in the future.

Taking this knowledge, I was able to begin my dream of opening a mental health practice in Malaysia, a country in need of mental health services and struggling to keep up with the needs of a nation coming out of a pandemic. Malaysia has also survived and been reshaped by racial tension, foreign occupation, and unprocessed generational trauma.

I began by studying the nation—working with the mix of Indian, Chinese, and Malay locals as well as the diverse group of expatriates from around the world. I noticed so many differences, yet just as many similarities in the pain of being unseen, in the effects of chronic stress or developmental trauma, and in coping with the absence of a good caretaker. I saw resigned acceptance of abuse, unquestioned and limiting gender roles, and more repression of conflict and emotion than I had witnessed in years practising in the US.

I have never met a person who does not have life experiences or knowledge they do not bury. We all have reasons to do so—it is an attempt to live the best we can. Without examining what we hold out of our awareness, we may miss out on the glory of living an examined life in which we understand ourselves. Only by facing the knowledge we have buried can we fully accept ourselves and see ourselves with the love and compassion we deserve. I invite you to read this book so we may begin this journey together.

Part I

How We Become Who We Are

Our foundations are laid before we open our eyes for the first time. Our creation involves epigenetics and intergenerational trauma, which are woven into our DNA and the ways in which our bodies function. Unknown to us, we are born with the information from our ancestors—inherited experiences and sensations. Studying what has happened to those before us allows us to feel connected to the experiences that join our families together in a created history. For the purpose of this book, we will start by learning more about epigenetics and intergenerational trauma to examine the past we have inherited.

Our development continues when we are born and begin our first relationships and experiences in the context of our families and primary caregivers. Thus, to learn more about how we become, we will focus on how our first attachments shape the way we trust, relate to others and the world, and create a framework through which we view our self-worth.

Chapter 1

Epigenetics

'Becoming is better than being.'

—Carol S. Dweck

Epigenetics: The Emotional Landscape We Inherit

There is nothing more reflective of a life buried and hidden than what we inherit genetically before we are even born. Many of us understand, to an extent, that our genes play a role in creating who we are. However, we are only beginning to understand the depth of how our family and environment prior to our birth create aspects of our life we are not aware of at a conscious level.

Even before the advent of epigenetics, the field of psychology recognized that our genes play a role in the mental health issues we develop, but there was no plausible explanation for how some of us seem to inherit the trauma and mental health of our parents and ancestors. Thus, much of psychology has focused on child rearing, parenting, and environmental factors to understand how a child develops mental health symptoms. Epigenetics has recently been gaining recognition for its staggering impact on how genes related to mental health, generational trauma, and emotions are expressed.

Recent research on epigenetics has extremely important implications about how our identities are developed and shaped through inherited trauma and stress.[1] This research on epigenetics has shown that parents' and grandparents' trauma and stress can be experienced directly by their children, explaining diagnoses of post-traumatic stress disorder (PTSD), long term stress, and chronic conditions long after a threat is gone. This is caused by the permanent alteration of the offsprings' genes in the womb or even as unfertilized eggs and sperms. We will explore the hidden imprint of trauma on our epigenetics and its implication on our mental health. Understanding this intricate relationship can pave the way for new interventions and approaches to support healing and resilience.

Epigenetics, in essence, is the study of changes to gene activity that do not involve alterations to the underlying DNA sequence. It is like adding annotations to the book of our genome without changing the words. Trauma, on the other hand, is an emotional or psychological response to an event or experience that is shockingly adverse, such as an accident, assault, or natural disaster.

At first glance, epigenetics and trauma may seem like vastly different areas. However, recent research has shown that trauma impacts up to three generations at a time.[2] The traumatic experiences faced by our grandparents and parents can leave marks on our psyche and epigenome, the plethora of chemical compounds that dictate how our genes are regulated. These epigenetic marks can influence how we respond to stress, our susceptibility to illness, and even the structures of our brain.

What Is Epigenetics? Decoding the Layers Beyond Genetics

Here comes the science. Feel free to skim past this if you are not interested in the nitty-gritty, but I encourage you to be open minded.

Epigenetics, a term coined by the biologist Conrad Waddington in the early 1940s, refers to changes in gene activity that do not alter the DNA sequence. The prefix 'epi' in Greek means 'above' or 'over', fittingly capturing the essence of epigenetics as the layer of biological regulation above the genome. It is about what happens on top of or in addition to the standard genetic process.

The Epigenetic Machinery

When delving into the connection between trauma and epigenetics, it is essential to shed light on the underlying mechanisms at play. There are several mechanisms by which the epigenome can modify gene activity. Epigenetic changes are principally orchestrated through DNA methylation, histone modification, and RNA-based mechanisms.

These changes might alter how someone reacts to stress or contribute to the risk of mental health issues.

These mechanisms have been explored in the following pages:

DNA Methylation

DNA methylation is one of the most extensively studied epigenetic mechanisms. It involves adding a methyl group (CH_3) to the DNA molecule, usually at cytosine bases. This addition can hinder the binding of transcription factors and, as a result, suppress gene expression. Among traumatized individuals, changes have been observed in the methylation patterns of the genes involved in the body's stress response. For instance, altered methylation levels in the gene regulating cortisol, a stress hormone, have been associated with experiences of childhood abuse. These changes can have long-lasting effects on how individuals respond to stress.

Histone Modification

Histones are protein structures around which DNA is wound, resembling beads on a string. Post-translational modifications of histone proteins, such as acetylation or methylation, can impact gene expression. For example, histone acetylation usually loosens the DNA around the histones, making genes more accessible and increasing their expression. Conversely, deacetylation leads to the condensation of DNA, rendering genes less accessible and reducing their expression. Traumatic experiences can induce changes in histone modifications, particularly in genes associated with stress response and neuronal plasticity.

RNA-based Mechanisms

Another facet of epigenetic regulation is RNA molecules. While DNA is the blueprint, RNA acts as the messenger and builder. Small RNA molecules, such as microRNA, can control gene expression post-transcriptionally. They bind to the messenger RNA (mRNA), destabilizing or blocking their translation into proteins. Trauma can influence the expression levels of these microRNA, which, in turn, can have cascading effects on a multitude of genes.

Crosstalk between Mechanisms

It is vital to recognize that these mechanisms operate in collaboration. There is intricate crosstalk among DNA methylation, histone modifications, and RNA-based mechanisms. This interplay can form a complex, dynamic network of gene regulation influenced by environmental factors, including trauma.

Understanding these mechanisms and their interplay is not just academically fascinating, but it can also potentially revolutionize our approach to mental health. With more profound insights into how trauma interacts with our epigenetic makeup, we can pave the way for novel therapeutic strategies to reverse or mitigate the epigenetic scars left by traumatic experiences.

Significance in Development and Cell Differentiation

Epigenetic regulation is crucial during development. Though many different cells in an organism have the same DNA, they can have vastly different functions (e.g., a neuron versus a skin cell). Epigenetics plays a central role by selectively turning genes on or off during development, allowing cells to specialize.

Adaptation

What makes epigenetics particularly enthralling is that it's an adaptable system. Unlike DNA, which is relatively static, the epigenome can change in response to the environment or lifestyle. For instance, diet, stress, and toxins can all induce epigenetic changes. This has far-reaching implications for health, behaviour, and susceptibility to diseases. It also is good news for those of us who are starting to understand the far-reaching implications of that which is buried in our genes, legacies, generational histories, and as we will see in future chapters, our minds as our lives are shaped. Knowledge of these intricacies is power—knowing more is better and arms you with how to intentionally use what you have to better your future.

Furthermore, there is evidence that the trauma, stress, grief, and anxiety experienced by a mother while a child is in utero and by up to two generations leading up to the child's birth lead to changes in the child's level of cortisol.[3] This is because the egg that forms the child in utero exists in the mother's body throughout her lifetime. Even before that, when the child's grandmother is only five months pregnant, the mother's eggs have already developed when she is in utero. Knowing this allows women to focus on their mental health and prioritize stress reduction during pregnancy. Having the field of epigenetics legitimized means providers know how to intervene and help women during pregnancy.

The Scope and Impact

Epigenetics bridges the gap between nature and nurture, offering insights into how the environment and experiences can shape an individual's genetics. Stress and environmental events leave marks on the methylation (aka chemical coating) of chromosomes, which 'becomes a sort of memory of the cell, and since all cells in our body carry this kind of memory it becomes a constant physical reminder of past events, our own and those of our parents, grandparents and beyond.'[4] Epigenetics can, therefore, foreshadow the chance of our children and grandchildren showing symptoms of stress or trauma—such as pain, hunger, intrusive memories, and more—due to our traumatic experiences and shared cultural experiences (like war or genocide). This genetic information is imprinted on us at the level of the eggs and sperms, setting up an unintended blueprint of memories related to a trauma we have never experienced and have no words for. We can use this information to nurture resilience and aid future generations in understanding what is impacting them before they are even born.

Epigenetics and Trauma

Over the course of their lifetime, 70 per cent of individuals worldwide will be exposed to traumatic events.[5] Trauma is an emotional or psychological response to an event or experience that is shocking, distressing, or harmful. Physiologically, experiencing trauma initiates a stress response that releases the chemicals cortisol, norepinephrine, and epinephrine while the person experiences a fight or flight response. The impact of trauma results in both physical and psychological symptoms that may manifest at the time when a trauma occurs or may be expressed later on in life.

There is a common understanding that facing a trauma impacts your functioning. However, the idea that your parents' and grandparents' trauma can be alive in you is a new concept. Based on the research of Bruce Lipton and Rachel Yehuda, pioneers in the field of epigenetic research, we now know that we are three times more likely to develop PTSD if a parent has PTSD and that individuals often show symptoms similar to the ones as their parents who have experienced trauma.[6]

How Epigenetics and Trauma are Connected

We have known for some time that trauma and genetics are related, just not how. Of the 50–85 per cent of individuals who experience traumatic events, about 30 per cent have a genetic component.[7] Research has shown that trauma can result in epigenetic changes.[8] The idea that we inherit the trauma of our parents through alterations in our genes has been brought to light by observing and studying everyone from the children of survivors of domestic violence and sexual abuse to survivors of collective trauma such as war and discrimination. These changes can affect how genes associated with stress and mental health are expressed, passing on transgenerational trauma. Essentially, trauma can alter how our genes work, which can, in turn, affect how we react to the environment and stress. Kellermann likens epigenetics to a computer system where the genome is the hardware and the epigenome is a variable software of memory files that function like a switch. Thus, the children of those who have experienced trauma and have PTSD are 'suffering from a software bug', which produces 'incorrect or unexpected results [. . .] which can inflict harm at certain unpredictable points of time'.[9] Despite the varied research on trauma and epigenetics, we are still figuring out the mechanisms at play and how they interact with each other. Clearly, the inherited trauma of our parents and ancestors can be debilitating to entire family lines to the point of rendering individuals unable to work or have healthy relationships.

One of the first major contributors to our understanding that trauma causes genetic changes comes from following up with individuals present during the terrorist attacks on 11 September 2001 in New York. The enduring stress and horror experienced by witnesses were found to particularly affect women.[10] Women who were pregnant at the time of the 9/11 tragedy were found to have babies with significantly lower birth weights and experienced premature birth at higher rates. Studies on women present during the 9/11 crisis showed that of 187 women who were medically checked for exposure to toxins, many had developed PTSD.[11] Among thirty-eight women and their babies who were followed up with nine months after the event, significantly lower level of the stress hormone cortisol was detected in their saliva. Cortisol is a stress hormone that helps the body activate the fight or flight response, get ready for danger, and come back to baseline after experiencing trauma. Specifically, cortisol is responsible for bringing down the increased adrenaline level during a potentially traumatic event, and it plays a role in both regulating arousal and forming memories of the event. If cortisol levels are too low then the body may not return to baseline, resulting in ongoing distress and traumatic memories. Over the course of studying intergenerational epigenetic changes, lower levels of cortisol have come to be associated with PTSD.[12] Surprisingly, shockingly low levels of cortisol were found in the saliva of infants born to the women who were present during 9/11 and developed PTSD. This effect was most pronounced among mothers who were in their third trimester of pregnancy during 9/11. Mothers of these children described them as more anxious overall and as having an increased fear of strangers.

Another collective tragedy—the Holocaust—has led to some of the most convincing research on the seriousness of genetic changes happening in response to trauma.[13] Like the children of women exposed to 9/11, adult children of Holocaust survivors have been found to have low levels of cortisol and high levels of stress hormones. This is important because prolonged exposure to stress hormones has been shown to weaken the immune system and cause issues such as hypertension. However, in the long run, low levels of cortisol indicate a higher propensity for the development of PTSD.

We have found that the children of Holocaust survivors have experienced anxiety, stress, and episodes and nightmares of reliving the trauma of being targeted, persecuted, and tortured by an enemy they have never encountered.[14] They are more likely to develop anxiety disorders and PTSD, and dysfunctional relationships.

According to research by Nathan Kellerman,[15] these individuals seem to have inherited the 'unconscious minds' and repressed trauma of their parents in a way that cannot be accounted for by parenting and child rearing alone. Descendants of Holocaust survivors reflect the memories of their ancestors through its imagery—the frigidity and the effects of starvation. Prior to learning about epigenetics, individuals were unaware of where these feelings, thoughts and experiences came from. They had no way of knowing these experiences; certainly not to the level of living them in their present. Can you imagine the shock and terror of experiencing such issues without context?

In response to these experiences, it makes sense that researchers like Rachel Yehuda have found that while descendants of Holocaust and 9/11 survivors have low cortisol levels, their parents have also developed lower levels of an enzyme responsible for breaking down cortisol. Research hypothesizes that reduced enzyme activity is a response to prolonged periods of starvation and threat to one's life because it allows for maximal storage of necessary glucose and reduced metabolic activity.[16]

However, the opposite is seen in the descendants of survivors who have low cortisol and high level of the enzyme that breaks cortisol down. According to Yehuda, this finding explains descendants being ill-equipped to survive in situations such as prolonged starvation and being more likely to develop PTSD or trauma related issues as a result. Furthermore, in cases where food insecurity is not an issue (e.g., concentration camps) and there is plenty of food, survivors are likely to have stress-related disorders like hypertension, insulin resistance, and obesity.[17]

Understanding the staggering impact of trauma on the lives of babies in the womb has turned our attention to the alarming possibility of the impact of psychologically distressing events—

such as discrimination, violence, natural disasters, and grief—by evaluating their impact on the birth outcomes of the exposed pregnant women. Not only does this impact individuals and their offspring but also has a huge potential to disrupt entire family lines and, at a larger level, societies.

Stress Response and the Hypothalamus–Pituitary–Adrenal Axis

Trauma typically activates the body's stress response. A key player in this response is the hypothalamus–pituitary–adrenal (HPA) axis. The HPA axis is a complex set of direct influences and feedback interactions between the hypothalamus (a portion of the brain), the pituitary gland (a pea-shaped structure located below the brain), and the adrenal glands (small, conical glands located on top of the kidneys).

When an individual experiences trauma, the hypothalamus secretes corticotropin-releasing hormone (CRH), which prompts the pituitary gland to secrete adrenocorticotropic hormone (ACTH). ACTH stimulates the adrenal glands to produce and release cortisol, a stress hormone. Cortisol helps the body cope with stress, but excessive cortisol release can harm the brain and body.

Epigenetic Regulation of the Stress Response

Epigenetic mechanisms play a significant role in regulating the HPA axis. For example, DNA methylation and histone modifications can influence the genes' expression in this stress response.

If an individual is exposed to chronic stress or trauma, the epigenetic regulation of genes associated with the HPA axis can change. For instance, changes in methylation patterns in the glucocorticoid receptor gene, pivotal for the functioning of the HPA axis, have been observed among individuals who have experienced early-life trauma.[18] Such changes can render the stress response hyperactive or hypoactive, contributing to psychiatric disorders such as depression, anxiety, or PTSD.

Epigenetic Memory of Trauma

The epigenetic changes associated with trauma can form 'cellular memory'. The cells may 'remember' the stress or trauma through these epigenetic marks, which can alter how individuals respond to future stressors. This is particularly relevant in understanding why individuals who have experienced trauma may have heightened or altered responses to stressors, even long after the traumatic event has passed.

The Neuro-Epigenetics of Trauma

The connection between epigenetics and trauma is intricate and profound. When an individual experiences trauma, it can instigate a cascade of biological changes. The body's response to trauma typically includes activating the stress response systems. This activation is essential, in the short term, for coping with immediate threats. However, when trauma is severe or persistent, this short-term adaptive response can have long-lasting effects on regulating genes that control these stress response systems.

It is also essential to look at the brain when looking at the relationship between trauma and epigenetics. Trauma can alter the epigenetic landscape of the brain cells. There is increasing evidence that epigenetic changes in neurons and other brain cells play a crucial role in learning, memory, and mood regulation.[19] These changes can affect synaptic plasticity, which is fundamental to the brain's ability to adapt and learn from experiences.

Altered synaptic plasticity due to trauma can mean the brain becomes more wired to recognize and respond to stress and danger, even when it is inappropriate. This can manifest as anxiety disorders, depression, and other mental health issues.

One of the critical aspects of the interplay of epigenetics and trauma is how trauma can affect the biochemical markers atop DNA. These markers are like switches that turn genes on or off, regulating their expression. Trauma can change the placement or presence of these markers, thereby affecting which genes are active or inactive.

For instance, consider the gene responsible for regulating the stress hormone cortisol. Under normal conditions, this gene maintains our body's response to stress. However, when trauma occurs, the epigenetic changes might alter the functioning of this gene, making an individual more susceptible to stress, which can contribute to mental health issues like anxiety and depression. DNA methylation is one of the primary mechanisms through which this happens. When a methyl group is added to a DNA strand, it can inhibit the gene from being read and translated into a protein, effectively turning it off. This process can be affected by trauma. For example, among individuals who have experienced severe childhood trauma, studies have found changes in DNA methylation of the genes involved in stress regulation.[20]

Similarly, histone modification is another mechanism by which trauma can affect individuals. Histones are the proteins around which DNA is wound, and they can chemically modify in response to environmental stimuli, including trauma. These modifications can affect how tightly or loosely the DNA is wound around the histones, affecting gene expression. For example, when the DNA is tightly wound, it's not accessible for gene expression.

The repercussions of these epigenetic modifications are vast and varied. They can affect an individual's mood, immune response, susceptibility to addictions, and even alter the structure and functions of their brain.

Understanding the interrelationship between epigenetics and trauma not only unravels the biological underpinnings of the impact of traumatic experiences but also opens doors to targeted interventions that might be able to reverse or mitigate these epigenetic changes.

In conclusion, the interplay between epigenetics and trauma is a dynamic and complex one that involves multiple physiological systems, especially the stress response and the nervous system.

Understanding this interplay can offer insights into the long-lasting effects of trauma and open avenues for interventions that address the epigenetic aspects of psychiatric disorders.

An Example of Trauma: Interpersonal Violence

To illustrate the changes in epigenetics due to trauma, let us look at one of the most common traumas experienced. Intimate partner violence (IPV) or domestic violence impacts about 20 per cent of women in the Western Pacific, 22 per cent in high income countries, and 33 per cent of women in Southeast Asia. It is defined by the Centers for Disease Control and Prevention (CDC) as violence that includes physical violence, sexual violence, stalking, or psychological aggression perpetrated by a current or former intimate partner.[21] We have long known that witnessing interpersonal or domestic violence impacts the developing brain and psychology of a child. The trauma of witnessing or experiencing other childhood adversities manifests among children in the form of a smaller prefrontal cortex and hippocampus. The prefrontal cortex is the part of your brain responsible for higher order decision making, planning, impulse control, organization, and problem solving, and the hippocampus is responsible for learning and memory. Both these parts of the brain being smaller means a growing child is more prone to learning difficulties, emotion dysregulation, aggressive behaviour, and them being wired for survival—not for thriving and connecting.

The unprocessed trauma of witnessing IPV stays buried within a child in ways they cannot process at a young age and leads to an increased risk of experiencing mental health issues, experiencing further violence, or perpetrating violence themselves at a later age. However, we must recognize that babies in the womb are also impacted by a mother experiencing abuse. Specifically, increased DNA methylation has been found among everyone from newborns all the way up to teenage children who have witnessed interpersonal violence.

DNA methylation variations on various genes are one of the most studied components of epigenetics, which has been found to be linked to early childhood stress and adverse events.[22] Particularly, epigenetic variation of genes operating in the HPA axis, such as the glucocorticoid receptor, have been found to be related to susceptibility to PTSD and impacted by the level of IPV experienced by a mother during pregnancy.[23] This is vital because the HPA axis is critical for homeostasis—it controls growth, reproduction, metabolism, and behaviour; it is also the primary line of the 'defence cascade' that helps humans deal with crises. Hyperactivity of the HPA axis can cause anything from a long-lasting head cold to depression. Hypoactivity of the HPA axis can cause undesirable consequences such as abdominal fat, loss of muscle mass, and mentally ill health.[24] It has been observed that these methylation changes impact children and even the grandchildren of those experiencing violence.[25] These changes are related to further impairments in learning, memory, and the development of mental health issues. The good news regarding epigenetic markers related to domestic violence is that early identification can allow us to work on pathways to building resilience against mental illness and focus on early detection and intervention.[26]

When discussing the connection between epigenetics and trauma, we explore the interface of environment and genetics. How does a traumatic experience, which is an external environmental factor, influence the internal workings of our genes? Let's unravel this by examining the stress response and its epigenetic regulation.

Epigenetic Changes and Future Generations: A Legacy

Interestingly, the epigenetic changes caused by trauma can sometimes be passed down to future generations. This means that the experiences of our ancestors can indirectly affect our gene expression. This phenomenon, known as transgenerational epigenetic inheritance, has been a topic of immense interest and research.

When epigenetic changes occur due to trauma, the alterations to gene expression can sometimes be passed on to the offspring. This means that children and even grandchildren may have altered gene expression due to traumas experienced by their parents or grandparents.

One striking historical example that has been extensively studied is the Dutch Hunger Winter, which occurred towards the end of World War II. People experienced severe malnutrition during this time. Researchers found that not only did children who were in utero during the famine have increased health issues, such as obesity and cardiovascular disorders, but even their children showed similar changes in DNA methylation patterns.[27]

This intergenerational transmission raises several questions about the inheritance of trauma. What mechanisms allow epigenetic marks to be transmitted to the next generation? How do these inherited changes in gene expression affect the health and behaviour of descendants? And can the cycle be interrupted or reversed?

In studies with animals, particularly among mice, researchers have found that experiences such as stress or exposure to toxins can lead to epigenetic changes passed down to future generations.[28] These studies often look at DNA methylation patterns or histone modifications and how they affect the expression of genes involved in stress response, metabolism, and other processes.

Intergenerational epigenetic changes represent a complex interplay between genetics, environment, and experience. They suggest that our health and behaviours might be influenced not just by our own experiences but also by the experiences of our ancestors. Moreover, this knowledge carries a responsibility—the awareness that our actions and experiences can shape the genetic legacy we pass on to future generations. It makes understanding and addressing trauma and its epigenetic effects even more imperative for the well-being of current and future generations.

Implications and Future Prospects

Understanding the interplay between epigenetics and trauma is promising for new therapeutic strategies—knowing how trauma can change gene expression, finding new treatments for mental health conditions, or better understanding how these conditions develop might be possible.

However, it's also essential to proceed with caution. The field of epigenetics is still young, and more research is needed to fully understand the mechanisms and their implications.

Ongoing Research in Epigenetics and Trauma

As the fields of epigenetics and trauma are ever-evolving, cutting-edge research is continually unfolding. Scientists and psychologists are delving deeper into the mechanisms through which trauma can leave epigenetic marks. Ongoing studies are exploring the potential for interventions that might alter these epigenetic changes, offering avenues for prevention and treatment. Furthermore, research about transgenerational epigenetics attempts to understand how the impact of trauma might cascade through generations. Technological advancements in gene sequencing and data analysis also propel this research forward. As we continue to amass knowledge, research about epigenetics and trauma synthesizing promises to revolutionize how we understand human biology and mental health, and how we approach treatment.

Chapter 2

Intergenerational Trauma

'Our wounds are often the openings into the
best and most beautiful part of us.'

—David Richo

Introduction

We understand the concept of intergenerational trauma as a reflection of our family's shared trauma, and the resulting shame, preoccupations, and reenactments. No one grows up in a vacuum. We enter the world and slowly learn our place in our family and society—all of which is influenced by race, class, financial stress, and how much we have suffered in response. Certain traumatic events impact us at a cellular level, as we have seen with epigenetics, and become a part of the legacy we are born into. When we talk about intergenerational trauma, we are talking about everything from historic events like war to family legacies of substance abuse. This trauma influences our physical and psychological make-up. Importantly, much of the knowledge and emotions associated with intergenerational trauma are unconscious till discovered. To reach our full potential, we need to understand the buried aspects of our legacies. Then, we can use this information to create the fulfilling life we are searching for.

When I ask people about their families, I get a mixed reaction. Some of them, I blame on how therapists on TV are always blaming mothers or unearthing repressed memories through sceptical means. However, I cannot overemphasize how much trauma becomes a legacy—passed on through our early childhood, affecting our attachment to peers and future lovers, and creating our sense of trust in ourselves and the world.

This chapter focuses on the creative and fascinating ways in which our minds cope with general and intergenerational trauma. Some may remember the trauma they experienced, while others may not—an interesting defence mechanism that protects us from feeling overwhelmed. However, learning what we have buried releases the power of negative emotions and narratives we live unknowingly. Often, this is where individuals are stuck in a cycle that is preventing them from feeling fulfilled, decisive, and purposeful. This chapter portrays the impact of intergenerational trauma though client stories of those who have found the power to embrace the trauma they were born into.

To understand intergenerational trauma, it is important to first have a basic understanding of trauma itself. Trauma is defined as:

> A disturbing experience that results in significant fear, helplessness, dissociation, confusion, or other disruptive feelings intense enough to have a long-lasting negative effect on a person's attitudes, behaviour, and other aspects of functioning. Traumatic events include those caused by human behaviour (e.g., rape, war, industrial accidents) as well as by nature (e.g., earthquakes) and often challenge an individual's view of the world as a just, safe, and predictable place.[29]

In essence, trauma is classically known as experiencing an event that is life threatening. It is normal for people to struggle with difficult thoughts, anxiety, sadness, anger, and experience a disruption of their normal lives for a period of time. However, according to the National Center for PTSD, 6 per cent of the US population will develop PTSD at some point in their lives. Specifically, about five in every hundred adults have PTSD in a given year. As of 2020, that's roughly 13 million adults a year in the US alone.[30] People's vulnerability to trauma differs significantly. There is lesser consensus about the statistics on PTSD and trauma in Southeast Asia, yet there is evidence that points to similar rates prevailing. For example, a study examining the impact of motor vehicle accidents in Malaysia found that 7.4 per cent of the respondents fit the criteria for PTSD upon follow up.[31]

Universally, women are more likely to get PTSD after experiencing a traumatic event than men are, with roughly eight in every hundred developing PTSD. Men, on the other hand, develop PTSD at the rate of four in every hundred. This rate was corroborated in Southeast Asia, where a study found one third of women experiencing symptoms of PTSD in the month following a motor vehicle accident.[32]

Dangers specific to certain regions and countries, as well as the types of jobs and lifestyles of individuals influence the type of traumatic events associated with the risk of PTSD. For example, in Southeast Asia, individuals are exposed to higher risk of natural disasters like typhoons, earthquakes, and tsunamis. Furthermore, political and social unrest, as well as the response and support provided by governments and society impact the risk of PTSD experienced in the region. In fact, the majority of research on PTSD in Southeast Asia has been conducted on wartime refugees and survivors who have faced genocide, displacement, and the conflict of war. Studies estimate that as high as 70 per cent of refugees hailing from Southeast Asia meet the criteria of PTSD after such experiences.[33]

Research has consistently shown that individuals working in dangerous jobs with relatively limited resources, such as veterans and emergency services, develop PTSD at higher rates than the average population.[34] There have also been times in history when PTSD has developed at higher rates such as after 9/11 and other acts of terrorism, and in times of war or limited resources like the Great Depression.

Taking this definition of trauma, we can now turn to the generational transmission of trauma and its effects. Intergenerational trauma is the transmission of trauma and its legacy to subsequent generations.[35] As we discussed in the previous chapter, much of this transmission is epigenetic, caused by changes to the chemical markers of a gene that result in consequences and adaptation to trauma. However, trauma can also be transmitted through parenting styles, the impact of parental mental health, and parents' responses to trauma. The children of parents who have experienced trauma can grow up to show increased shame, guilt, feelings of helplessness, anxiety, depressive disorders, substance abuse, experience difficulties with emotional regulation, and struggle more to maintain stable relationships. This is said not to cause shame or anxiety about the impact of trauma but rather to bring solace in the knowledge that these are reactions to trauma that point to great suffering and that there is help available to overcome this pain.

Historical Trauma

In the previous chapter, we saw that surviving the Holocaust left a mark on the genes of subsequent generations. Looking at the psychological impact of transgenerational trauma, we see that the mental health of the adults who survived historical and collective trauma as children changes throughout their lifetimes. Much of the research following individuals across multiple generations has been done on Holocaust survivors. So, we will use it as an illustrative example. Specifically, the adult children of Holocaust survivors have been shown to experience significantly higher rates of anxiety, grief, guilt, unhealthy relationships, and intrusive thoughts and images related to the Holocaust. These individuals often do not understand what is happening to them, as their lives have a completely different context than their grandparents and parents.

Growing up, individuals are often aware of their parents' or grandparents' legacies related to the Holocaust. Information is shared, a story or narrative of the struggles an individual's family has faced and persevered through is formed. Often, gratitude and themes of working hard to build an exemplary life and family are passed down through these stories as expectations for the children to live up to. However, the children of survivors are hearing stories, not experiencing these atrocities. They can empathize but do not have the conscious knowledge that comes with the lived experience of the fear of persecution, the muscle memory of starvation, the experience of being torn away from loved ones, or the other horrors experienced by survivors of the Holocaust. Despite this, adult children have been reported as stating that while they only remember pieces and disjointed stories of their parents' and ancestors' war stories, they have always felt the weighty presence of the Holocaust in their family home.[36]

On the other hand, not having this lived experience means they do not have the connection to a community built around honouring the experiences of the survivors and providing support. Often, individuals feel at odds with the narratives and experiences passed down to them. They feel the staggering impact of the undefinable trauma their ancestors have experienced but are helpless to make sense of it and understand how to process and resolve the related emotions.

The power of emotional safety, connection, and community has been repeatedly proven through research.[37] This is similar to how the therapeutic relationship provides a safe person and space to witness and facilitate a person resolving trauma with hope and strength.

From what we have learned about the parenting styles of Holocaust survivors, they display increased levels of detachment in parenting and a resultant increase in disorganized attachment among their children.[38] This means that individuals who survived the Holocaust or other major trauma are more likely to be emotionally unavailable due to their own grief, mental health issues, and health problems. It is understandable that individuals who have survived such horrific trauma face the risk of being more detached as parents because traumatized individuals tend to have higher levels of hypervigilance, dissociation, anxiety, depression, difficulty regulating emotions, and may meet the criteria for a PTSD diagnosis. Individuals—no matter how caring, loving, and devoted as parents—may struggle to connect with their children for some time to their entire lifetime because their struggle to overcome the horrific event they endured takes up their emotional resources.

We will cover attachment in the next chapter, but for our purposes now, attachment can be thought of as the quality of the relationship between a child and a caregiver. If a child consistently has their needs met, they develop secure attachments, which means growing up trusting the world, a lower risk of mental health problems, and tendency to have healthy, caring relationships during their lifetime.

A child who develops disorganized attachment does not have their needs met consistently as an infant. Instead, they struggle with developing trust, as their needs are met unpredictably, and they cannot predict if and when their caregivers will meet their needs. Sometimes, caregivers meet their needs. At other times, their needs for connection, food, diapering, attention, and more are unattended. This teaches a child that others are not predictable and cannot be trusted all the time. A child, thus, reacts with their own mixed signals when bonding. They may reach out to be picked up only to scream when their mothers do so. They may cry when their father leaves the room, only to ignore him when he returns. Unfortunately, this type of detachment can be common among individuals who are struggling with their own mental health issues and grief, despite trying their best to meet their children's needs. A child in this situation is not met with the expected looks of adoration, smiles, and encouragement on their caregiver's face that encourage a bond to flourish.

Growing up, this dynamic sets the stage for the level of security in and health of relationships experienced as an adult. Thus, survivors of historical trauma, such as the Holocaust, experience more dysfunctional and chaotic relationships. Especially since they may be unaware of the trauma buried in the histories of their ancestors and the consequent stifling of connection, communication, and emotional availability stemming from trauma.

Other research has described the transmission of trauma to subsequent generations of Holocaust survivors as occurring through parents' post-traumatic adaptational styles.[39] Post-traumatic adaptation style is defined as, 'a way of life that becomes an integral part of her/his personality, repertoire of defence or character armour, view of oneself, of others, and of the world. They become a style of being in the world. They often also influence parenting and affect the children's psychosocial development and adaptation, thereby becoming intergenerational.'[40]

Individuals were found to be stuck in various degrees of 'fixity', which block the free flow of the concept of time from their past to present to future as a response to their own trauma.[41] Yael Danieli describes four post-traumatic adaptational styles: numb, victim, fighters, and those who made it.[42]

An individual's post-traumatic adaptation style is found to shape parenting and, consequently, their children's upbringing, emotional development, identity, and beliefs about themselves, people around them, community, and the world. Importantly, individuals whose parents have both survived the Holocaust were found to have more post-traumatic symptoms than those who have a parent who survived the Holocaust and married someone who did not have the same experience. This is likely related to having one versus two parents who may struggle from emotional unavailability and detachment caused by the denial and silence surrounding the collective trauma of the Holocaust. This points to the protective benefits of having at least one emotionally available and stable adult in a child's life.

In terms of specific post-traumatic adaptational styles, a survivor who fits in the 'numb' category perpetuates a legacy of silence. This survivor isolates, seeks connection infrequently, and struggles with a low tolerance to stimulation. They tend to be minimally involved in the lives and caretaking of, and bonding with their children before hitting their emotional limit. At this point, they retreat from the situation and their family. Their children are left to figure things out in the absence of an active parent.[43] Children may misinterpret this parenting style as a lack of interest and caring. This leaves a critical opening for connection in the child's life as they search for something or someone to fill the void of the parent, causing a vulnerability to risks, such as substance abuse and predators, or negative affiliations such as with gangs or other unsupervised children. This is where having a supportive community or another trustworthy adult can make a pivotal difference in a child's life by providing connection and guidance in addition to their home life.

People who feel like victims because of their post-traumatic adaptation style are distrustful and suspicious of the world and others. They adopt the worldview that others are out to get them and, as a result, often make turbulent caregivers who are often depressed and feel hopeless and helpless. Fighters use their experience and strengths as their armour against the world, finding it difficult to let their guard down for others at the price of connection. They are strongly driven to build, achieve, and succeed, and fight against any sign of weakness or self-pity. Lastly, people who fall under the category of 'those who made it', manage successful socio-economic lives and seek to maintain their status. However, this is done by distancing themselves from their trauma and their connection to other survivors to prioritize their goals of higher education and political and social achievement.

Other research has supported Danieli's, as well as pointed to other parenting behaviours such as overprotectiveness, rejection, irritability, anger, and parentification.[44] The importance of understanding a parent's response to trauma is to understand their parenting obstacles with compassion and the purpose of providing informed care and intervention.

Let's take another example of collective and historical trauma. In the late 19th century, governments of Australia, Canada, and the USA operated under the principle that it was best for society to 'assimilate' aboriginal and native children into local culture by removing them from their communities and sending them to residential schools. Studies[45] on aboriginal individuals removed from their homes and subjected to residential schools have found that they faced incredible losses at the hands of individuals attempting to erase an entire culture and devastated entire generations' sense of identity and meaning.[46] Studies involving aboriginal descendants describe the following two generations as 'lost' because these individuals who were removed from their families were also removed from their cultural values, traditions, and legacies.[47] They were disconnected from not only their sources of comfort and familiarity but also their heritage and community. Since that moment, these individuals have been living with this trauma and have felt a void of connection to family and community that they may not be able to fathom or verbalize. These individuals have expressed lacking a sense of belonging and connection to their ascribed language, customs, spirituality, and practices while feeling abandoned by caregivers who had no say in these traumatic separations.

Many of these individuals left these schools and went on to build families of their own—a daunting task when you do not know where you came from. As a result, these survivors took their buried, unprocessed, and unspoken trauma and handed it to the generations that came after them.

The forced assimilation of and discrimination against Native Americans has been found to be largely responsible for the issues faced by them today such as high rates of suicide, interpersonal and familial violence, and substance abuse. The anger and confusion stemming from the abandonment they felt from their families and caregivers has resulted in anger taken out at their own future families, resulting in chronic physical, sexual, and emotional abuse and violence in the family home.

Interestingly, children and grandchildren of those forced into residential schools have been found to be more present rather than future oriented. This follows from individuals who do not identify with a past or lack the structure and guidance of family and community in shaping the values, customs, and meanings of their futures. While the residential schools provided a system to live in, they did not provide meaning and fulfilment. Without a way to own their past or envision their future, these individuals were more likely to fall prey to unhealthy coping mechanisms, such as alcohol and substances, while not knowing how to create and maintain healthy relationships and stable careers. In fact, follow up studies[48] have found that subsequent generations tend to have limited connection and contact with their nuclear and extended families, since they are more likely to have absent family members or those preoccupied with drugs and alcohol.[49] At the community level, Putnam describes that Native American individuals suffer from a lack of social capital such as trust, reciprocal relationships, and social engagement.[50] Other research focuses on the great loss to the Native American community through a lack of transmitted skills, knowledge, support, and opportunities.[51] These lost generations point to the importance of uncovering knowledge and emotions associated with trauma. Doing so allows for connection and building resilience, both of which are tremendously difficult when you do not know the extent of what you have lost.

The evidence around transgenerational impact of trauma continues to multiply, and it has horrifying implications.[52] The descendants of Ukrainian individuals who lived through Holodomor have been similarly impacted, with children growing up to report high levels of disconnection from their community, mistrust, strict and rigid parenting, anxiety and depression, as well as issues such as hoarding, overeating, increased risky behaviours, and feelings of shame and guilt that have also been seen among the children of individuals who have been imprisoned, such as Holocaust and genocide survivors.[14] Furthermore, the impact of collective trauma is far reaching among refugee populations and those who have suffered due to slavery and discrimination, such as African Americans.

Let's take the example of Ibrahim. He was a fourteen-year-old boy I met working at a community health centre aiming to help Iraqi refugees who had been persecuted due to their religion. Ibrahim's family included his father, mother, and two sisters. His two other siblings did not make it to the USA with them, as they were killed before they had a chance to escape. Ibrahim was quiet, bright but subdued. He had been taken from his home and community where he had known little stability due to the lack of safety in his surrounding environment. In some ways, he was lucky that he had no memory of the conflict and destruction that he faced in his home country, as he had left as a little boy, prior to the age of four when memories cannot be recalled or verbalized.

However, he carried the trauma of the loss he had seen around him and his mother's distress, grief, anxiety, and PTSD when she had been pregnant with him in his non-verbal memory and body. His family on both sides were no strangers to life endangerment and a constant lack of safety. They hoped that escaping to a town in north-eastern USA would restore their sense of safety, calm their constant sense of distrust and anxiety, and allow them to build new lives. In fact, they relied on the changes they expected would come from living in a developed country.

However, like many who live for survival and have no room to reflect on emotional needs, they were unaware of the emotional and psychological toll of their trauma, which started manifesting when they reached safety. Ibrahim slowly found that his mother felt unreachable and preoccupied. While loving and patient, she was prone to withdrawing to her room and spending hours, sometimes days watching the news of her family and friends back home, reliving the horror they had experienced every day in new ways. He could hear her crying and felt badly about burdening her when he needed lunch, help with his homework, or a simple hug.

Ibrahim's father, on the other hand, seemed to carry all of the anger in the world. He also watched the news but did so late at night when his mother was not around. Ibrahim did not understand the sadness and anger his parents carried, but he felt them, as these emotions were like ghosts in their house.

He could not remember a life in Iraq or the family and friends they had lost. They were names and stories to him. Instead, he was dealing with the very real challenges of being a fourteen-year-old boy, navigating anxiety and symptoms of trauma he had never been warned about and had no name for. Over the course of the next few years, Ibrahim struggled to gain attention from his parents and learned from his peers what to value and prioritize in his life. He found a girlfriend who he felt peace and belonging with for the first time in his life and threw himself into this relationship. This simple relationship made him feel the normalcy and excitement of being a teenager in high school, which he had craved.

His parents continued to be detached from his life. They were overly permissive out of a sense of guilt instead of guiding and parenting Ibrahim in a country that was difficult for even them to navigate socially. Ibrahim's dependence on his girlfriend worked against him because he rationalized her demeaning language, growing aggression, and mood swings as something he should help her with instead of calling it out as the abuse that it was. When he came back to see me after a few years at the age of nineteen, he was caught in an abusive relationship, which he struggled to recognize because of his loyalty and more so because he could imagine tolerating abuse over returning to isolation and his buried needs for connection. He could not imagine anything more for himself.

It took a long time to untangle Ibrahim's reluctance to accept that he was in an abusive relationship and trace it back to him being neglected in childhood and the trauma he had inherited from his parents and grandparents. These were areas of his past he was unwilling to look at, convinced that he should be stronger than the experiences of his parents. He rationalized that many kids have parents who are not present and that he should enjoy his freedom. His parents tried their best, after all, and loved him and his two sisters dearly. He greatly empathized with the reasons they could not be present and felt that, as the oldest boy in the household, he should put his sisters' needs before his own. This belief was deeply ingrained in him by the age of nineteen, confused and buried with Ibrahim's difficulty in accepting his own needs. Deep down, he knew something was wrong, but it is hard to put a name to feelings you have never been taught to identify. Left unattended, Ibrahim was heading down a path of accepting relationships that hurt him, and never asking for more for himself when it came to work, friends, or fulfilment.

Therapy for Ibrahim began with educating him about the symptoms of intergenerational trauma he experienced—hypervigilance, dysregulated emotions, a sense of impending doom and fear, and most importantly dissociation when faced with emotional challenges. Ibrahim, like many trauma survivors, disconnected from strong negative emotions and felt foggy and unbalanced.

In this state of mind, he lost time easily, particularly when faced with a problem he had to solve. To help him, we worked on grounding skills to cope with the dissociation and trauma symptoms. We then confronted the impact of his parents' numb and fighter post-traumatic adaptation styles. Ibrahim learned to understand that he could have empathy for his parents' struggles while also grieving the loss of attachment and connection he had experienced growing up. Ibrahim was able to slowly differentiate himself from his parents' struggles as refugees and internalize that he should expect more for himself. He learned to respect his needs and be compassionate to himself, to let go of toxic narratives related to putting others first and being a man.

Years later, he still has moments where he instinctively buries his needs or gets lost in the trauma he inherited, but he is able to gain perspective quickly and move forward. He is a triumphant example of why we need to understand how intergenerational trauma holds us back, but if we work through it, we build resilience and connect to our strength and parts of our character that we never became familiar with before. It is through our early experiences that we see our value and learn our strengths as reflected back by our caregivers. When detached parents deny those opportunities, we have to independently learn how to value ourselves and be resilient. This is where therapy can help most to repair the impact of intergenerational trauma.

Adverse Childhood Experiences

Collective and historical trauma have a widespread impact on specific populations that is felt for generations. However, humanity as a whole faces equally threatening and impactful issues on a daily basis, just often behind closed doors. These issues are categorized as adverse childhood experiences (ACEs) and are defined as any potentially traumatic event that occurs during the ages of zero to seventeen—from experiencing violence, abuse, or neglect;

witnessing violence in the home in the form of interpersonal or community-level violence to having a family member pass away by suicide.[53] This definition also includes the impact of family members or the household struggling with substance abuse, mental health issues, and trauma and/or the child experiencing food, economic, or safety insecurity and instability.

As you can imagine, ACEs impact a large percentage of people from any community. Research based in the USA shows 64 per cent of the adults there have had an ACE while one in six adults have experienced more than four.[54]

Given these statistics, it is likely that you may have experienced an ACE yourself. Below is a simple assessment you can take to find out:

What Is Your ACE Score?

The ACE questionnaire is a simple scoring system that attributes one point for each category of ACE. The ten questions below each cover a different domain of trauma and refer to experiences that occurred prior to the age of eighteen. Higher scores indicate increased exposure to trauma, which has been associated with greater risk of negative consequences.[55]

During the first eighteen years of your life:

1. Did a parent or other adult in the household *often or very often* swear at you, insult you, put you down, or humiliate you? *Or* did they act in a way that made you afraid that you might be physically hurt?
2. Did a parent or other adult in the household *often or very often* push, grab, slap, or throw something at you? *Or* did they ever hit you so hard that they left marks on your body or injure you?
3. Did an adult or person at least five years older than you *ever* touch or fondle you or have you touch their body in a

sexual way? *Or* did they attempt or actually have oral, anal, or vaginal intercourse with you?
4. Did you *often or very often* feel that no one in your family loved you or think that you were not important or special? *Or* did your family not look out for each other, feel close to each other, or support each other?
5. Did you *often or very often* feel that you didn't have enough to eat, had to wear dirty clothes, and had no one to protect you? *Or* were your parents too drunk or high to take care of you or take you to the doctor if you needed that?
6. Were your parents *ever* separated or divorced?
7. Was your mother or stepmother *often or very often* pushed, grabbed, slapped, or had something thrown at her? *Or* was she *sometimes, often, or very often* kicked, bitten, punched, or hit with something hard? *Or* was she ever repeatedly hit for at least a few minutes or threatened with a gun or knife?
8. Did you live with anyone who was a problematic drinker or alcoholic or someone who used street drugs?
9. Was a household member depressed or mentally ill? Did a household member attempt suicide?
10. Did a household member go to prison?

For each question you answer yes to, you add one point. Your score is the total of these points. The higher the score, the higher the risk someone has of developing physical and mental health issues later in life. Thus, the more someone's ACEs, the more mental issues they report having as adults.[56] We will explore what an individual's ACE score and experience of early trauma mean for them under the chapter on trauma.

In the context of intergenerational trauma, it is important to know that the children of parents who experienced ACEs have consistently been found to have poorer physical and mental health, to struggle with more developmental issues, and to have more difficulty with socioemotional issues. If both parents have experienced ACEs, the risk of mental illness is significantly higher.[57] As we have discussed, the risk of PTSD, specifically, can be passed on from one generation to the next, which partly happens because of modifications to DNA methylation and epigenetic changes. However, like other mental health issues, it can also be caused by parenting styles, perpetuated abuse in the household, and interpersonal and environmental changes resulting from a prior generation's trauma.

Interpersonal Violence

One of the most studied ACEs is interpersonal violence, also known as domestic violence. It has impacts as far reaching and dramatic as catastrophic events like 9/11 and the Holocaust. By definition, interpersonal violence refers to physical, sexual, or psychological abuse by a current or former intimate partner and is the most common form of family or household violence.[58] One in three women worldwide experience interpersonal violence in their lifetimes, while one in four to one in eight children grow up in a household where interpersonal violence is inflicted at some point.[59]

In general, growing up in a violent household increases an individual's risk of both experiencing interpersonal violence and perpetuating it against their own partner or children[60] and developing social, emotional, mental, and physical health issues. Specifically, children who witness interpersonal violence have increased difficulties—such as absenteeism, poorer grades, withdrawal from other students and teachers, as well as behavioural problems (like acting out, aggression towards peers), anger, depression, and anxiety—in school.[61]

Most children are unable to emotionally process the trauma of witnessing violence, especially if they are below five years of age. As we will learn in chapter four, trauma is stored in a child's bodily memory even if they are pre-verbal or under the age when they are able to form and recall memories. Even if they are able to recall and verbalize what happened, interpersonal violence, like most traumatizing events, is surrounded by a culture of secrecy and shame. Thus, most children do not share what is going on in the household with outsiders. In fact, for therapists, the first signs of something being wrong at children's homes are changes in grades, withdrawal from friends, and changes in behaviours at school. Most children are alone when they face violence between their parents, struggling to comprehend how someone they love could also hurt another person they love. Such children may feel helpless in their own home, angry or fearful about the abusive parent, and disconnected from or worried about the abused parent.

While they may never directly face violence (although many children from violent homes do), they absorb the impact of the trauma and react as if they have experienced it directly. Kids display the same symptoms as the parent experiencing violence—intrusive thoughts, nightmares, or flashbacks about the trauma, avoidance of certain people and places, anxiety and depressive symptoms, fear, hypervigilance, and difficulty regulating emotions. In fact, children at the age of four have been found to already consistently exhibit emotional and behavioural issues if they come from a violent household. Not everyone experiences the same symptoms, but if children exhibit the behaviours mentioned above along with behavioural changes at school and around friends, there may very well be something wrong in their homes.

The effect of a child witnessing violence between parents is passed on to the subsequent generations.[62] This happens due to a cycle of problems beginning in the parent–child relationship. Specifically, a child who witnesses a parent being abusive has more difficulty establishing healthy relationships as an adult. This happens due to the impact of trauma and a healthy relationship between adults not being modelled for the child. Subsequently, the child witnessing such traumatic events finds it difficult to bond with their kid, creating an unhealthy attachment and parent–child bond.

Knowledge about this pattern is important because studies have shown that up to 51 per cent of adults have witnessed violence in the home and almost half (42.9 per cent) of them have reported poor physical and mental health as a consequence in adulthood.[63] Some studies estimate that up to two thirds of children in homes with interpersonal violence develop behavioural, cognitive, and psychological problems in some form.[64] There are some gender differences in the way children respond to interpersonal violence. Women, or our future mothers in this situation, are more likely than men to experience physical and mental health consequences upon witnessing interpersonal violence. Furthermore, men who perpetuate witnessed violence are more extreme in their violence than women who perpetuate violence. The fact that women are impacted the most mentally and physically portrays a stark truth. Not only are these women more likely to have complicated pregnancies and be at risk of the violence but they also have to contend with the physical and mental transition and burden of becoming a mother to a new child.

It is important to note at this juncture that interpersonal violence might be expressed through violence but is actually about the abuser asserting power and control over their partner and family. Most women who become pregnant have little control over the decisions relating to their body, including whether they want to or can have a baby, when they seek medical attention, and whether they can access support during pregnancy and child rearing. It is in the abuser's best interest to keep their partner isolated from family and friends to keep the abuse a secret and maintain control over the person. Along with isolating the victim, the abuser retains strict control over the victim's finances and any aspects that can prevent the abused from leaving the relationship, such as immigration papers or their children's documents. Thus, the mother in this situation often feels helpless and hopeless about her ability to care for and raise a child. She is often dealing with her own responses to trauma, the reality of her limited opportunities and circumstances, as well as the growing fear over her child's safety.

This can easily bleed into the mother's relationship with her child once it is born. Some women may instinctively maintain a barrier between them and their child, knowing that they do not have control or power over how their child is raised, leading to detached or overly permissive parenting. Others may struggle too much with their own physical and mental health issues to be able to connect properly with their child. Coupled with their children's increased risk of developing PTSD and mental health issues from the epigenetic changes caused by their experiences, the beginnings of these children's lives already constitute a struggle in ways that need intervention.

Take, for example, Lydia. She came to see me as a twenty-three-year-old who was struggling with anxiety about her current relationship. Lydia had trouble trusting her partner and found herself becoming easily suspicious and angry at him. When she started to feel suspicious, she became extremely dysregulated emotionally and would say things she regretted. She told me that she felt like she was abusive in her relationships, which greatly bothered her because she had experienced abusive relationships and came from a family with a legacy of intergenerational abuse. When we started to dive into this disclosure, we found that her relationship was suffering from the intergenerational trauma of her mother's parenting and its impact, helping Lydia acknowledge her abuse and holding the teacher who abused her accountable.

As a sixteen-year-old, Lydia was in a relationship with a teacher at her school. At the time, Lydia did not know that anything wrong was happening with her. She lived in a country where it was normalized for younger girls to be with men who were inappropriately older than them. And, after all, her teacher, Tom, did not seem 'old'. He was a young teacher who enjoyed going out to bars. All the girls in her class thought he was cute and cool. So, when she met Tom during a night out at a bar, she felt excited and thrilled about the encounter. She had never been told by her parents what a normal relationship should look like, especially for a sixteen-year-old girl. In fact, her parents did not talk to her about anything important, let alone relationships and sex or warnings about how tricky and smooth predators can be.

Lydia knew she should not talk about her new boyfriend, but it was not a well-kept secret either. Her parents were aware she was seeing someone and assumed that he was from her class. Growing up, Lydia's mother was also traumatized by the different men she dated. She belonged to a generation that was even more likely to keep interpersonal violence a secret, classifying it as a family issue that should not be spoken about. Lydia's mother did not have any good models of women who were treated well. So, she assumed that most women put up with the situations as she did. She could not imagine a different life for herself or her daughter.

While Lydia's mother cared greatly for her daughter, she was never shown or considered a different style of parenting. She tried to support her daughter in the things that made her happy but did not consider the things she was failing to protect her from.

One day, suddenly, when Lydia's mother was called to Lydia's school, she was surprised to find out that her daughter had been dating a teacher. However, something strange happened. Lydia was adamant that her relationship was different, and that she was not being taken advantage of. Meanwhile, Lydia's mother got to know Lydia's boyfriend and thought he was a good man who was not with her daughter because of her age. Due to her blind spots towards predatory relationships rooted in her abuse, Lydia's mother allowed the 'relationship' to continue. She rationalized the relationship and found herself believing her daughter's insistence that they loved each other, finding it increasingly difficult to see Tom as anything more than a man unwillingly caught up in a difficult situation.

Years later, Lydia realized that she had been in a predatory relationship and saw Tom for who he really was. At the beginning of therapy, she had already realized that her and Tom's relationship was inappropriate and that he abused his power to take advantage of her. However, she only just started grasping the levels to which she was groomed and preyed upon. She was even more unprepared for the realization of how her parents and other adults around her failed to protect her.

This led to a period of tension between Lydia and her mother. Lydia had decided to press charges against Tom and began a self-led process of navigating the legal system. During that time, she had to ask for her mother's cooperation to file charges and for other legal pursuits. Plus, at an even deeper level, she craved for her mother's validation of her traumatic relationship and wished for her mother to recognize her mistakes. She wanted the healing experience of her mother standing up for her and saying that the relationship had been wrong and apologizing for not protecting Lydia by intervening when she should have. Instead, her mother furthered her conflicted feelings of guilt, shame, and pride over pursuing justice by voicing her reluctance about participate in the proceedings. Furthermore, her mother was frequently sympathetic to Tom, as he had his own family by then. She seemed reluctant to ask questions or encourage her daughter to pursue justice. She never offered an explanation or expressed willingness to even discuss the subject.

As you can imagine, the lack of validation by her mother hindered Lydia's progress in therapy and led to her going back to having panic attacks. Lydia had triumphed over much of her past by acknowledging and processing the abuse she suffered and its impact on her choices in subsequent relationships. Specifically, she found that she tended to be attracted to older men who, while she admired their accomplishments and maturity, often made her feel insecure and dismissed her daily struggles and anxiety. Unintentionally, Lydia was repeating the model of the relationship she had experienced, and her mother before her had also lived. However, unlike her mother, Lydia started questioning her role in her unhealthy relationships. It would have been easier to turn away from the problem and continue to blame the men she dated. However, Lydia was also a resilient and self-aware individual. Over time, she started taking accountability for her own trauma reactions in relationships, realizing that the anger and dysregulation she felt were products of the abuse she had faced. She learned to regulate her emotions and tolerate her distress better.

Lastly, she began to realize that she had to break the cycle by choosing different men, which was most difficult. She would not feel the same connection to such men initially because they lacked the thrill and excitement she felt with older men. But, they offered her a way to reprogramme her relationship model and achieve a healthy relationship.

Lydia's mother's lack of support and validation at pivotal moments made Lydia second guess her move towards a different kind of relationship and value system for herself. She doubted herself and wondered whether she was exaggerating Tom's behaviour by calling it abuse. Even worse, she wondered if people thought she was playing the victim and seeking attention over made up problems.

As you can see, we could not have understood Lydia's difficulties or helped her in therapy without exploring the role of intergenerational trauma. Doing so, we were able to help Lydia reparent her needs for validation and develop a healthier relationship model, understand the aspects of her mental landscape that she inherited from her mother, and make different, empowered choices toward a healthier future for her and her future children.

As Lydia's example proves, there is much value to understanding beliefs arising from narratives of interpersonal violence and trauma. Those who have experienced violence in the household are more likely to perpetuate violence against their spouses, children, or even parents. The vast majority of cases of violence against parents are boys being abusive towards their mothers.[65] In these cases, it has been theorized that boys who witness the tactics of power and control exerted by their fathers against their mothers model the same tactics. This indicates a rupture in the mother–son bond that often involves difficulty seeing the mother as someone to be respected. The child learns that violence is an acceptable way to approach conflict and to influence solutions to get a desired outcome. Mothers of abusive boys describe their children being used as weapons in the father's attempts to control, influence, and undermine them. Consequently, the boys directly witness the name calling, belittling, and minimization of their mothers' humanity. Often, these mothers are even more likely to keep their sons' abuse secret, as they feel personally responsible for the failure to protect their children in such situations.

Children who grow up experiencing interpersonal violence most commonly abuse their own partners or children. This occurs due to reasons similar to the ones discussed above. Growing up, these children are shown that aggression is the most effective and appropriate way of getting their needs met. Furthermore, power and control over another person is structurally normalized in a relationship. Obeying someone's rules and answering to their needs at the cost of one's own is mistaken for love and support. It is difficult to break this ingrained pattern, as the abusive adult child has been shown only this way of expressing love, and one's perception of love is a powerful thing.

We have focused on interpersonal violence as the dominant example of the impact of ACE on a child, even in terms of intergenerational trauma, because it is one of the most researched and well-known issues. However, ACEs in general impact the next generation through poor physical and mental health. This is particularly alarming because violence has a cumulative impact. The more types of violence or potentially traumatic events a person faces, the more the next generation is impacted too. Since we know that experiencing a kind of trauma makes one more likely to experience another kind of trauma, we can see multiple ways these facts are significant and worrisome. Given this knowledge, we can identify families and individuals who are at multiple levels of risk to provide education and supportive intervention.

I shared this story in the hope that people recognize the value of learning and understanding the totality of what impacts us. We are formed from the blueprint of the epigenetics created by our parents' experiences. We all feel unnamed anxieties and discrepancies in our lives that we cannot explain. We may know that our parents have faced traumas and difficulties that we cannot fully fathom but that does not help us specifically identify the ways these issues have impacted us. In therapy, we know that the first and hardest step is being able to identify and acknowledge the reality of the problems we face. Doing so reduces the power of these buried elements and gives us workable problems that we can tackle in the light of day. Understanding ourselves is a way to bring forth resilience and reduce the impact of our blind spots.

Chapter 3

Attachment

> Oh, the glory of it all.
> Was lost on me,
> Till I saw how hard it would be to reach you.
> . . . and I'd always be lightyears away from you.
>
> —'Lightyears', The National

The mystery of a satisfying, meaningful, and lasting relationship is a problem that eludes many of us. Many an individual has walked through my door to ask, 'Why am I broken when it comes to relationships?' People from all walks of lives—particularly those who are smart and capable, with close relationships to friends—struggle with the concept that they can be desirable yet unable to have a successful relationship. Some of them start to notice patterns, whether in the ways they react, the type of people they date, or in the way relationships end, leaving them with an all too familiar, all-encompassing feeling of loneliness and emptiness. This is where the concept of attachment theory comes in. It explains the impact of elements of our childhood and our earliest relationships, which we may have buried for the sake of self-preservation.

A whole early life of formative memories and knowledge is just an arm's length away in our subconscious, shaping every relationship, what we struggle with, and how we communicate and manage our emotions and conflicts. Understanding the life and knowledge of buried attachment helps us piece together the glory in us all—what we bring into our relationships and how we can choose to move forward in them.

What We Bring to Our Relationships

Our self-worth, the way we learn to interact in relationships, and how much we trust the world, ourselves, and others is determined by our early attachments to our caregivers. This concept is called attachment theory. It states that if we have positive experiences with parents who consistently and predictably attend to our needs, nurture us, and protect us, we feel secure about ourselves and in our relationships.[66]

This concept is not to be underestimated, as it is the primary way we learn self-worth and trust in the bubble of our family as an infant. As humans, we like to create and reuse templates for organizing our experiences to predict future situations and relationships. These early experiences act as blueprints for how we interact with others and predict how they will treat us.

As infants, we rely on our caregivers to fulfil our needs and to show us what social connection looks like. That's why we have mirror neurons in our brains geared specifically towards growing our neural networks by imitating the observable actions of our caregivers. So, if we see love, adoration, and nurturance in our caregiver's behaviour towards us, mirror neurons are fired to reflect these behaviours. They continue to do so as we repeat these behaviours in the future. A child who sees love and nurturance becomes accustomed to associated behaviours and similarly is more likely to engage in such behaviours. Thus, recognizing our worth and place in this world begins by reflecting what we see in our caregivers' eyes and actions. An infant who sees love and adoration in their mother's eyes, reacts by developing a sense of worthiness and security about themselves. Additionally, if an infant is distressed and cries, and a parent consistently picks them up, soothes them, and attends to their needs, they learn that people and the world in general can be trusted. These behaviours, in turn, lead to the infant developing behaviours that encourage bonding, like smiling, reaching out, and reacting positively to connection. This carries on far past the boundaries of the home, resulting in a child who connects in positive social ways with new friends and individuals.

If a parent is unavailable emotionally or physically and fails to provide comfort and security when an infant is ill, distressed, or in need, they feel uncared for and unseen. They may cry and protest when they are in need but after days and months of their cries going unanswered, they learn to conserve their energy and not bother anyone. The evolutionary purpose of protest behaviours (gaining protection and nurturance) becomes obsolete.

Thus, it is important to understand that our experiences in the first few years of our lives determine how secure we feel about ourselves and others throughout our lives.

The first six months of a child's life are especially important, as infants are able to predict their caregiver's responses by this age. Yet, we do not have a conscious memory of the first three years of our lives. This phenomenon, called infantile amnesia, occurs because our hippocampus is not fully developed till after the age of two, which means that some of our most formative memories are buried deep inside of us. Many of us can downplay the impact of these early years because we don't have memories from that time, but we may feel an uneasiness and loneliness that cannot be effectively explained despite various attempts to move forward. This is because the insecurity and needs buried deep within us are alive in our implicit memory and show themselves in our everyday lives, the way our bodies and minds function, and how satisfied we feel with our lives and relationships.

Attachment Theory Explained

Based on studies of infants and their mothers, John Bowlby developed the attachment theory, a conceptual framework to explain the importance of parents meeting their children's social–emotional needs. When Bowlby conceptualized attachment theory, he was intrigued by the perceived impact of children and their mothers being separated during the Second World War. At the time, his research was controversial, as the thinking on child development back then was that children are shaped by the way they handled their internal conflicts and drives.

Bowlby's stance brought to light an opposing view that external events, particularly parents' responses to children's needs became the basis for healthy identity and relationships. Bowlby established that infants are innately motivated to seek closeness and proximity with their caregivers.[67] Infants do this through proximity-seeking behaviours like crying, cooing, reaching, and clinging. These behaviours serve the purpose of regulating their emotions and facilitating their basic needs (eating, being changed, sleep) being met. In the same way, infants exhibit protest behaviours when their caregivers leave, as their sense of security disappears, with the absence of their caregiver representing a secure base to explore from.

Over time, if their needs are consistently met and they are protected and nurtured by their caregivers, infants become more comfortable with exploration and trust that separation from caregivers will end with them being reunited. This is the basis of building basic trust, a process that is difficult to learn later in life, although it is quite automatic in the early months of life. Children whose parents neither respond to them positively nor meet their needs consistently and predictably or nurture and protect them, develop a negative internal working model of themselves (a negative view of themselves). The social and emotional needs of these children are not met. Thus, they protest and learn alternate ways of communicating their distress to their caregivers.

Put another way, the four attachment styles can be seen as organized or disorganized. The first three—secure, anxious, and avoidant—fall under organized attachment. Anxious-avoidant attachment falls under the umbrella of disorganized attachment. This may sound surprising, but it makes inherent sense if you think about it. In the organized attachment categories, children learn there is an appropriate way to react based on their caregivers' predictable reactions. For example, a child with a secure attachment style knows that their needs will consistently be met. They only exhibit protest behaviours (i.e., crying) if their distress goes unnoticed or they need attention. Similarly, for children with anxious or avoidant attachment styles, parents also react in a particular manner consistently, even though it is not healthy or nurturing. Therefore, the child also learns to respond in an adaptive, preservative way. For example, if a parent is avoidant of a child's distress and expression of needs, they adapt to minimize outward displays of emotion, crying, and gestures of closeness. This is adaptive in terms of survival, as there is a predictable pattern to their parents' rejection, which the child, in turn, adapts too.

However, children with anxious-avoidant attachment styles are simultaneously learning to use avoidant or anxious behaviours in close relationships with others. Suppressing emotion may be helpful around caregivers who reject closeness in relationships, but it does not aid that child when they attempt to build relationships with others later in life. Instead, they are perceived as cold or distant and have difficulty communicating how they feel, which jeopardizes their chances of developing genuine connection and safety in relationships. These buried emotions and attempts at closeness with early caregivers become disconnected from our awareness. This leads to such people losing out on the glory of a genuine relationship with flaws, difficulties to work through, safety, and unconditional acceptance.

Attachment has a far-reaching impact on the biological, social, emotional, and relational development of a child. Experiences repeated through infanthood strengthen associated neural networks in the brain. The repeated events, emotions, behaviours, and thoughts experienced through infanthood and childhood lead to associated neurons being inhibited, pruned, or expanded. Over time, a child develops inner stories and working models about themselves such as 'I am worthy of love' or 'No one can be depended on.' These are key lenses that we filter our experiences through in a manner that confirms and grows these working models, regardless of whether they are correct. We actively seek out experiences that confirm our worldviews and avoid unfamiliar experiences that go against our working models. Understanding inner working models, cognitive schemas, and the stories we create about ourselves is the subject of chapter eight. Targeting these narratives to understand our inner, buried, and made-up stories is the central component of cognitive behavioural therapy, which allows us to build healthier ways to interact with our lives, relationships, and selves.

While John Bowlby conceptualized attachment theory, Mary Ainsworth brought it to life with her research on mothers and infants in the 'strange situation' experiment. In the experiment, an infant's interactions with their mother and willingness to explore a new situation when a stranger is present are observed. The theory underlying the experiment hypothesized that the mother represents a secure base. So, infants with 'secure' (or healthy) attachment feel safe to explore and play in new situations in their mother's presence. Thus, the security an infant (or one-year-old, in this case) feels in the presence of their mother increases trust and independence while approaching new experiences and people.

These new experiences, in turn, become the building blocks of trust in ourselves and others.

A second component of the experiment looked at the infant's reactions to their mother leaving the room, and their subsequent reactions when she returned. Based on this study, attachment research evolved to understand that individuals can be categorized as those with secure or insecure attachment. Furthermore, people with insecure attachment are characterized by avoidance, anxiety, or a mix of both in relation to others.

In the strange situation experiment, it was found that infants with secure attachment explored new situations, while checking in with their mothers. They protested when she left the room and responded with excitement and physical closeness when she returned. However, those categorized as having anxious attachment were unwilling to leave their mother's side, could not be consoled when she left the room, and exhibited crying and clinginess upon her return. In contrast, those with avoidant attachment seemed somewhat uninterested in their mothers and explored new situations without reconnecting with her. Their behaviour did not change when she left the room or returned.

Finally, the last attachment style is categorized as disorganized or anxious–avoidant attachment. Babies in this category oscillated between clinging to their mothers and rejecting her attempts to console them. The information gained from the strange situation experiment captures both the impact of early attachment, nurturance, and protection between parents and kids, and shows how these bonds teach children how to approach new experiences and people. Children who learn that they can safely explore their environment with the guidance of their caregivers have the gift of expanding their horizons while staying safe. Those who cannot rely on their parents for safety may stop themselves from exploring the world, meeting new people, and growing past their current circumstances.

You may wonder what your own attachment style is. Below is an assessment to guide you in understanding your own attachment style. Do not be surprised if you do not fall neatly into a category, for things are not black and white when it comes to ourselves and our lives. We will explore each attachment style further until you understand the worldviews and reenacted behaviours, thoughts, and patterns you have developed to protect yourself. It is important to remember, at this juncture, that some of us have been taught to enjoy the closeness and comfort of relationships whilst others have been taught to manage relationships in terms of self-preservation. Be gentle with yourself if you feel yourself pulled towards the latter. A lot of guilt and shame can lie in the actions and reactions associated with thinking about relationships in terms of self-preservation. This is particularly the case for children who have experienced abuse or neglect and, thus, have struggled to maintain relationships with caregivers to survive. Much of the impact of disrupted attachment occurs outside a child's awareness without them understanding the depths to which a caregiver should be responsible for their well-being. Instead, children try to appease caregivers, walk on eggshells around potentially explosive moods and substance issues, and act in ways that make their caregivers more likely to look favourably upon them and provide the nurturance and connection they so need.

Revised Adult Attachment Scale: Close Relationships Version

The following questions concern how you *generally* feel in *important close relationships in your life*. Think about your past and present relationships with people who have been especially important to you, such as family members, romantic partners, and close friends. Respond to each statement in terms of how you *generally* feel in these relationships.

Please use the scale below by placing a number between 1 and 5 in the space provided to the right of each statement.

1	2	3	4	5
Not at all characteristic of me				**Very characteristic of me**

1) I find it relatively easy to get close to people. _____
2) I find it difficult to allow myself to depend on others. _____
3) I often worry that other people don't really love me. _____
4) I find that others are reluctant to get as close as I would like. _____
5) I am comfortable depending on others. _____
6) I don't worry about people getting too close to me. _____
7) I find that people are never there when you need them. _____
8) I am somewhat uncomfortable being close to others. _____
9) I often worry that other people won't want to stay with me. _____
10) When I show my feelings for others, I'm afraid they will not feel the same about me. _____
11) I often wonder whether other people really care about me. _____
12) I am comfortable developing close relationships with others. _____
13) I am uncomfortable when anyone gets too emotionally close to me. _____
14) I know that people will be there when I need them. _____
15) I want to get close to people, but I worry about being hurt. _____
16) I find it difficult to trust others completely. _____
17) People often want me to be emotionally closer than I feel comfortable being. _____

18) I am not sure that I can always depend on people to be there when I need them. _____

Scoring Instructions for the Revised Adult Attachment Scale

This scale contains three subscales, each composed of six items. The three subscales are *close, depend,* and *anxiety*. The *close* scale measures the extent to which a person is comfortable with closeness and intimacy. The *depend* scale measures the extent to which a person feels they can depend on others to be available when needed. The *anxiety* subscale measures the extent to which a person is worried about being rejected or unloved.

Original Scoring Instructions

Average the ratings for the six items that compose each subscale as indicated below.

Scale	Items
Close	1 6 8* 12 13* 17*
Depend	2* 5 7* 14 16* 18*
Anxiety	3 4 9 10 11 15

* Items with an *asterisk* should be *reverse scored* before computing the subscale mean.

Alternative Scoring

If you would like to compute only *two* attachment dimensions—attachment *anxiety* (model of self) and attachment *avoidance* (model of other)—you can use the following scoring procedure:

Scale	Items
Anxiety	3 4 9 10 11 15
Avoid	1* 2 5* 6* 7 8 12* 13 14* 16 17 18

* Items with an *asterisk* should be *reverse scored* before computing the subscale mean.[68]

It is important to note that your attachment style does not arise solely from your relationship with your caregivers. While most disruptions in attachment resulting in insecure attachment styles are the product of early childhood experiences with caregivers, there are other factors that can be significant contributions. Some of the most influential factors are temperament, genetic predispositions, mental health, trauma, and interpersonal relationships and events. This will be discussed further throughout the book.

Four Types of Attachment

Secure Attachment

This is what we are all aiming for—the kind of attachment that brings out our most comfortable and confident selves. If you have secure attachment, you have a relatively easy time trusting others or picking up on when someone is being disingenuous with you.[69] Although you may worry about some aspects of yourself, you generally have a good sense of self-worth and believe that if you work towards something, it will turn out well.

Relationships are healthy when you are with a secure partner because you are able to openly discuss needs, wants, and complaints without burying them or feeling guilty for having them. Because of the straightforward nature of a person with secure attachment, their partners feel respected even when there is conflict in the relationship, and they can see a path forward to resolve issues.

Anxious (Insecure) Attachment

Someone with anxious attachment has been shown that they cannot consistently rely on anyone.[70] Growing up, their caregivers sporadically respond to their needs for protection, comfort, and nurturance. The key here is that the parent responds enough for the child to learn that they need to react more loudly and expressively to be heard. At the same time, they learn to tune into the subtle shifts in a parent's mood or behaviour to actively have their needs met. A good example is parents who have issues with alcohol or substance abuse. Such parents might be responsive and caring towards their child until they are intoxicated or suffering from withdrawal (a hangover), in which case, they may dismiss their children or become easily angry and irritated, causing their children distress. If they drink excessively, even daily, their children become used to parents who they cherish in sobriety and are flooded with distress, disappointment, and feelings of loneliness when they drink.

Take the example of Natalie. She and her two siblings had a cold, distant father, and a mother who was joyous, spontaneous, and loving towards her and her siblings. Natalie remembered the family putting on plays together, cooking fun and creative dinners, and spending time playfully enjoying each other's company. Natalie shared that her father had not always been cold. In fact, he used to be affectionate and spend time with the rest of the family. But when Natalie turned nine, her father said she was too old to be cuddling with her parents or showing affection. He rejected and abandoned her in her eyes. This was followed shortly by her older brother leaving the house for college. She had looked up to him as another caregiver, who protected her from kids in the neighbourhood and school and took interest in playing with her. She was stunned when he went to college and never returned. She was entirely unprepared for this loss. She felt abandoned and intensely unloved by the two main male figures in her life.

This was only the beginning for Natalie, as she at least had her fun, loving mother. She had no idea that her mother would change following her brother's departure and would start drinking more each day. For Natalie, times of play and spontaneity were punctuated by changes in her mother's mood as she became more intoxicated. At first, these times felt unexpected and out of character, as her mother became angry and critical, lashing out with words that Natalie could not comprehend coming out of her mother's mouth. All too soon, she became used to her mother turning into this other version of herself. Natalie came to know the subtle signs that her mother was drinking. Frequent trips to the bathroom or kitchen, becoming increasingly sentimental, and pulling away from her kids and withdrawing into herself. Natalie never got over the deep well of hurt over losing her mother in this slow, insidious way.

When Natalie grew up, she married a man. When she reached the same age her mother had been during the issues they faced together, Natalie found her own behaviour changing accordingly. She became sensitive and reactive to the shifts in her husband's moods. Everything from the abruptness in his voice to every time he seemed to glance at his phone for work resulted in a dramatic shift in her mood and happiness. She reacted pre-emptively, shutting down or lashing out. See, her thwarted relationships with her parents and older brother had showed her what it felt like to feel safe, comforted, and protected by someone only for these things to be pulled out from under her. No matter how much reassurance her partner offered, Natalie struggled to move past the insecurity of a betrayal being around the next corner. It took time, but Natalie began to realize that she was not seeking reassurance from her partner, she wanted to trust herself to know that she had understood her earlier betrayals and could release herself from these reenactments.

Avoidant (Insecure) Attachment

Someone with avoidant attachment has learned through early experiences that others cannot be trusted—when they are vulnerable, they will be let down and disappointed.[71] A child with avoidant attachment often has caregivers who are neglectful of their needs and fail to protect them despite wanting to. Often, these individuals find that their caregivers reject or abandon them when they express high levels of emotion or need. This teaches them that suppressing and burying emotions is the best way to get their needs met and avoid disappointment.

Having avoidant attachment does not mean that these individuals do not have friends or avoid social contact. In fact, they often have quite high self-esteem and are empowered by their lack of dependence on others. This freedom allows them to connect with others easily in certain situations yet struggle to surpass a certain depth of intimacy. It is only when relationships become vulnerable and intimate that they pull away. For example, they may know how to charm and make a potential partner feel special. Dating can be easy, as can taking steps to further the relationship. However, often, avoidant partners have 'phantom exes' who they compare their relationships to or view as idealistic partners, and they are unable to accept the partners they have. You may be intuitively familiar with the concept of a phantom ex. In essence, a phantom ex is a person from one's past who, over time, comes to be the idealized standard for all partners and relationships. As a result, one continues to compare new dating partners to the phantom ex until they find a flaw that is considered a deal-breaker. Relationships with avoidant partners often feel like you are helping your partner 'get over' an old relationship but are not good enough for them to surpass their unresolved issues.

Avoidant partners pull away during times of vulnerability and commitment. For example, you may go on a wonderful vacation together and talk about the future, share vulnerable feelings, and come back full of hope for the relationship unfolding . . . only to be met with sporadic messages and ambiguous plans to meet next.

The avoidant partner wants closeness but begins to pull away when they get it. If you are the person with avoidant attachment, your behaviour might baffle you. Think back to how your attempts to be close and vulnerable to others have turned out. Were you hurt or disappointed? Were you only loved on the condition of achieving certain grades or performing well in a certain way?

The avoidant partner needs to make the choice to trust and relearn that they are worthy of love and acceptance without arbitrary conditions. Intimacy means vulnerability and, at times, may be uncomfortable, but it results in the rewarding connection the avoidant partner has longed for.

Disorganized (Anxious/Avoidant) Attachment

The only disorganized category of people who have anxious and avoidant attachment react unpredictably to intimacy and commitment in relationships. They are raised by caregivers who sometimes protect them and meet their needs and other times, they do not.[72] Sometimes, a parent could seem like the childhood hero and other times, like they had no connection to them at all. People in the disorganized attachment category develop deeply buried feelings of inferiority, abandonment, and rejection. They struggle to have a consistent, stable sense of identity and tend to have chaotic relationships as a result. Individuals in this category might seem disinterested in connection or downplay their needs in relationships. However, often, when unseen, they are anxious about and preoccupied by their relationships and just have no means of communicating this.

The caregivers of individuals who fall in this category can be a range of things from neglectful to sexually, physically, and/or emotionally abusive. In the case of abusive parents, children learn that their primary provider of safety is also hurting them and instilling fear in them. This learning is carried into adulthood, creating a vulnerability among adult children of abuse who feel familiarity in toxic or abusive relationships.

To understand attachment in the context of traumatic relationships, let's look at Scarlett. Scarlett is a thirty-six-year-old Asian woman who came to me because she was struggling with sadness, loneliness, and emotional pain, leading to frequent suicidal thoughts and, on the worst days, suicide attempts. Scarlett did not have any tools to make herself feel safe. Triggered by a feeling of loss or abandonment, something buried deep within her would awaken and flood her with thoughts of her being worthless, disgusting, and shameful. She was transported back to being a five-year-old, who she pictured cowering in the corner of a closet, not knowing who she was or who she could be. In those moments, Scarlett was lost in the hate, abuse, and neglect she experienced at a primal level as an infant and child. She felt the helplessness and inability to escape that she felt as a child accompanied by the name calling and hatred she felt for her father. In these memories, her mother stood by passively as her father physically abused her and, as we will later discuss, carried out her own damaging behaviour through manipulation and inducing feelings of guilt and obligation in Scarlett.

Scarlett, like many survivors of early childhood trauma, had more difficulty remembering her early years than expected. It is expected that most children will remember things by the age of four, when their hippocampus is developed and they are able to use language. This means that earlier, pre-language experiences shape us but are not consciously recalled. Scarlett, however, was neglected when she cried, squirmed with hunger, felt lonely, wanted to play, or needed to be changed—a baby's immediate, most basic needs. Suppressing these needs goes against the natural order of things and is a learned behaviour.

Try to think of your first memory with your mother. Close your eyes, imagine as vividly as you can what it feels like to be in that memory. What do you feel? For Scarlett, that memory is of her mother scolding her for being unable to use a cooking appliance she was not even old enough to handle. The most striking part is that Scarlett, like most children who survive abuse, face their abuse in private, never realizing that they should not feel like they do or that they deserve better.

As I write this, Scarlett is in the hospital following a suicide attempt. She desperately felt that she needed to have a connection with someone in a moment when she could not have one. That moment overpowered everything she had built in her life and reduced her vision to the painful loneliness she tried to bury inside her. For people like Scarlett, it is hard to hold on to the fact that people love and care about you when buried deep inside is the larger, terrifying fear that you are not worthy of love and that it can disappear at any moment. Still, the love and concern of a friend saved her life, even if she could not imagine what love and protection were in that moment.

Attachment: What Does It Mean for Adult Relationships?

We have learned that those happiest in relationships have secure attachment styles. This group roughly comprises about 50 per cent of the population.[73] The good news is that our attachment style is fluid and can change over the course of our lives based on our relationships, experiences, and choices. Entering secure, loving relationships strengthens our sense of trust and security in the world, our partners and, in turn, ourselves and our self-worth. Such relationships impact us at a physical level, as having secure partners helps regulate our blood pressure, heart rate, breathing, and levels of hormones in blood[74], in addition to aiding our mental wellness. However, it is important to note that 'security' can often be missed in a relationship if we do not work on ourselves and understand our past relationship trauma. The glory of the relationship cannot be appreciated if one tries to avoid its flaws in all aspects. Growth and security in a relationship are not possible without uncovering the buried knowledge of past relationships and attachment patterns and piecing together who we are in a relationship.

Take Anna for example. She came to see me with her partner Mark for couples therapy. When they first walked in, they seemed like a loving, supportive, and affectionate couple. Right away, they told me that they had a very positive relationship in every way and were only here for one problem they could not solve—Mark did not want to have children. Through the course of couples therapy, we explored why Mark did not want to have children. In this case, Anna believed that the reasons Mark did not want to have children were buried in childhood experiences gone awry. However, as we slowly unearthed aspects of their relationship, it turned out that Anna had buried her needs and disappointments under the belief that reaching a compromise over having children would fix their relationship.

Anna and Mark disappeared from therapy and, after a while, Anna returned alone, having broken up with Mark. The person I saw in front of me was a different Anna from the one I had seen before—gone was the agreeable, mild-mannered woman. Instead, here was someone who felt much more real—sad, frustrated but real.

Anna expressed that a statement from a previous session had stuck with her and planted a seed in her mind—her needs and dreams were also a priority, and that it was okay for her to take space in her relationship; both partners are the main characters of their shared story.

While she did not know it during the session months ago, that seed took roots, and she began to see what she had buried under her false certainty that the relationship's only issue was a workable disagreement about having kids. Buried under it, she discovered that there was a core issue of feeling that she was not a priority in Mark's life, that he had thought of a whole life without considering that they would build a life together, sharing happiness, dreams, and goals. Instead, Mark could only foresee being the main character of his own life for reasons he did not want to uncover.

Once Anna realized there were issues she was blind to in the relationship, we uncovered that buried even deeper were the pervasive questions at the core of her being—why had she not seen the faults in their relationship? Why had she unquestioningly played the supporting role to Mark's 'main character' for so long? The answer hit her like a sledgehammer—Anna had been playing the role she had her whole life, following the model presented to her by her parents and even more damagingly so, her father.

Anna's father had a larger-than-life presence. He was a focused career businessman who looked after his family. He built a family business and generously employed and financially supported his family. He held power and control over his immediate and extended family and failed to recognize that his children needed love, attention, and nurturance. Anna did not know that her father had buried a legacy of pain arising from his parents and grandparents. She just knew of her resentment and anger towards him. Why then, she asked as she realized this, could she own her anger towards her father but had always made her way to men who acted the same way? Why had she acquiesced unknowingly?

This moment of reckoning happened when Anna started to understand the life she had buried, only to reenact the attachment injuries of her past. Sigmund Freud calls this 'repetition compulsion' or a tendency for people to reenact their early traumas in an attempt to master the situation and create a different outcome.[75] Repetition compulsion can occur in different forms but is related to the early trauma or attachment difficulties that someone is unable to express. The trauma, whether it is a tense relationship with a parent or early abuse, is buried in a person's unconscious in an attempt to protect them. In many instances, the person is able to discuss the facts of the traumatic events from their past but buries the emotions and pain associated with them, and consequently is unable to process and heal from the trauma.

Examples of repetition compulsion include repeating abuse, choosing partners who are distant or cold if a parent was emotionally distant growing up, or experiencing flashbacks and nightmares about past abuse.

You may relate to Anna or Mark or begin to feel curious about the roles you repeat in relationships. Clients often come to therapy seeking to further their knowledge of themselves after struggling through a bad break-up and realizing that their relationships feel all too familiar, following a troubling pattern. Often, a recent relationship is the last straw that makes a person with buried trauma feel overcome with paralyzing feelings of loneliness, despair, rage, and a deep sense of abandonment. These may be accompanied by urges to fix the relationship at all costs, lash out at their ex-partner or themselves, or drown their emotions in medication, alcohol, food, or work. For some, these emotions and urges are so raw and overpowering that they are unable to function or go about their lives because everything seems trivial in comparison.

Claire, another client, came to see me after cutting off contact with an on-again, off-again relationship. She had an urgency I am accustomed to seeing in someone who is in pain over losing a relationship, and, worse, has realized that the toxic ex is not the only one to blame, that they are also culpable in creating the toxic situations that play out regularly in their relationships. Claire, a professor, is an insightful, smart, and capable woman who realized that she was happy with her life, work, and in her friendships, but that none of that mattered when her partner, Jordan, was upset at her or, worse, was non-committal and evasive. As usual, we began talking about the relationship Claire was in, paying attention to early warning signs that triggered feelings of unease, how Claire reacted (second guessing then dismissing herself), followed by the tumultuous relationship that was built up in jagged steps.

Claire met Jordan on a dating app. She was single and content, performing well at work and enjoying where she was in life. She had been through complicated relationships in the past and had decided to give that part of her life some space. Yet, sometimes, she felt curious about who was out there. One day, Claire decided to meet Jordan, who she had exchanged some messages with and figured she had nothing to lose by meeting him for a drink. Little did she know that what she expected to be a fun night out would end with her being stood up. At this point in her story, Claire jumped forward to a few weeks after the first date on which she was stood up, when she received a message from Jordan, out of the blue, at 10 p.m.—not a good sign. It was his birthday, and he asked her to come over, spend time with him and his family. A baffling message and invitation from someone you barely know and who had made a poor first impression. To add to the confusion, Claire decided to go and ended up having an electric, momentous night with Jordan, celebrating his birthday, surrounded by his family for a small get together.

That night sealed Claire's fate. Her anxious attachment style led to feelings of closeness and intimacy while unconsciously ignoring alarm bells attached to the mixed messages she had been receiving. What followed was a hot and cold relationship. She described the times they were physically present in each other's company as perfect, but the times in between as chaotic and unpredictable. Jordan did not want a commitment, he voiced it strongly, but in person, he acted with possibility and hope that the specialness of their connection could mean more.

Claire reflected feeling constantly berated, put down, and shamed, with pockets where Jordan shone his light on her and pulled her back in. Late night phone calls, chance encounters, and seemingly magical nights kept their relationship alive on a series of highs, despite its bleak reality. Claire described reaching the point of no return in their relationship several times, with Jordan yelling at her after he behaved horrendously, only to turn the blame back on her. You may be wondering why a smart, savvy woman like Claire was seeing Jordan. In fact, many of you may have friends like Claire or may be like Claire—caught between knowing Jordan's behaviour is wrong, that he is not going (and does not want) to change, and the inexplicable urge to fix him.

She explained to me that their relationship ended when he admitted to being with someone else after two years of gaslighting her into thinking she had imagined the signs, that the story about him leaving with another girl, reluctantly shared by a cousin, were untrue. He confirmed her fears out of the blue—on a call at 3 a.m. from a bar on the day she lost her job. Her emotional turmoil that day was already known to him, as she had reached out to him first for support. I'll let you ponder what that unprovoked attack during one of Claire's lowest moments says about Jordan's attachment style. Going back to Claire, she dealt with the shock of this betrayal while grappling with the mind-blowing accusations about Jordan's behaviour being provoked by her. He had been looking at this girl during one of her family member's wedding. After noticing several glances between Jordan and the mystery girl, Claire had angrily said, 'Why don't you just go speak to her if you're going to keep looking at her?' So, he did. He spent the next forty-five minutes speaking to her—as Claire's shame, embarrassment, and sense of disbelief grew—all while surrounded by family and friends. Claire ended up leaving, hurt and without intention of returning. However, this was not the end of their story. Jordan insisted that nothing happened after Claire left. But then, he dropped the bombshell that something did happen because she had basically 'dared' him to do it and sealed the deal by leaving.

What followed was a period of disconnection . . . until they reconnected. This time, he pulled her in by inviting her to a wedding (of all things!) where she met his friends for the first time. This had been a huge point of contention in their relationship and was probably the only concession that led Claire to pause and reconsider. He gave her that, and it was enough to restart things. One day, he reached out to her to say he was not romantically interested in her, that he just cared about her as a friend. Claire asked Jordan to block her to stop her from reaching out to him in a moment of weakness so that she could finally move on with her life. She admitted to me that, in the past, every day she was away from him came with an almost overpowering urge to reach out, to fix things, or just reconnect one more time. This can be attributed to Claire's anxious attachment style, the need to reconnect under any means necessary. The wound of the person you are connected to abandoning you, leaving you, is more painful than the harm of reaching out.

Jordan, however, refused to block Claire, saying she should be the one to take that step. Days later, he went as far as to begin messaging her again. He is a classic example of an avoidant attachment style. He reached out when she tried to separate, and he felt confined by the intimacy of the relationship. He ended things and when she accepted this, he restarted the relationship. The relationship restarted only for it to rapidly implode, with Jordan disproportionately blowing up at Claire's mistake. What is interesting here is Jordan not being able to tolerate Claire trying to move forward on her own terms. He needed the narrative of their relationship to end because of something Claire did, not because of his mistakes or lack of desire to commit and sustain intimacy with someone.

What is even more interesting is what Claire told me next. She shared that in the end, Jordan was yelling at her in public, drawing the attention of those around. He blamed her for the spotlight being on him, for how heinous her behaviour was. Meanwhile, she tried to fix the situation, to sit calmly and let him vent his frustration. When he tried to leave, she felt desperate that he stay because him leaving would mean the end, and she could not tolerate that. This is where the most pivotal statement about Claire comes in—she confided that she felt like she was trying to 'claw her way back into his heart' every time. She did not even realize she said it. Actually, through every encounter she shared, Claire never once mentioned the pain she felt or any emotions at all. At this juncture, she finally expressed an emotion to me, saying that she felt helpless, small. She kept repeating the word small. I asked her what being small reminded her of. Whose hearts had she tried to claw her way back into? How helpless and small was she in those memories? With startling clarity, Claire recalled being a child and being yelled at and criticized by her parents. Being told that she had to be a certain way to be their daughter, learning slowly that love was conditional. She learned that love had to be earned and maintained and that if something happened to anger someone, it was because she caused it and had to fix it. Claire had not been able to own any of these buried feelings—in fact, she had described her childhood as 'perfect' and continued to be close to her parents.

Her relationship with her parents had changed over the course of her life. They appeared to grow more understanding and less confrontational but, in reality, she learned how to act to get their approval. However, she buried the memories and feelings she had as a helpless child, trying to claw her way back into her parents' hearts, deep in her non-verbal, implicit memory. She described the tension in her body as she spoke and could explain fragments of her memory to me. However, the emotion was disconnected. Now that we had realized the life and connection Claire had buried, we could unearth it, examine how it impacted each of her relationships and kept her in a pattern of reenacting the need for unconditional acceptance. We could see the stark reality that Claire had attempted to gain the same approval from Jordan by clawing her way into his heart. To break her pattern since childhood, we would have to unearth the fragments of her memories, emotions, and bodily sensations from her unconscious and connect them to a cohesive story of a girl who was taught she did not deserve love and respect but that she should spend her life trying to earn it at the expense of her own self-worth.

It is important to note that your mind has fascinating and creative ways of trying to protect you, especially when you are young and dependent on others and cannot physically escape or change your circumstances. However, the defence mechanisms that protect you in childhood, become less useful over time as we develop more agency and competency in adulthood. We will discuss defence mechanisms and maladaptive coping in more detail in chapter seven. For now, it is important to note that defence mechanisms keep distressing information from the unconscious and prevent someone from moving forward, connecting memories with unhelpful thoughts, disavowed emotions, and confusing bodily sensations. Repetition compulsion, for example, does not create awareness, meaning the cycle of trauma repeats without true mastery over or closure of the early trauma. It is still buried under layers of the unconscious, waiting to be truly unburied so the person can intentionally choose how to connect with someone.

However this chapter made you feel, I encourage you to step away from your attachment pattern and see what emotions, bodily sensations, and thoughts emerge. We will now discuss trauma and the events that can shape our lives in a direct and unpredictable manner. We will return to attachment later in the book to integrate what we are born with and what happens to us along the way. Remember, we are always seeking the knowledge, sensations, and emotions that we have buried. While this can be a painful path to go down, this knowledge is already part of you and can be used to finally feel the acceptance you need.

Part II

That Which Shapes Us Along the Way

So far, we have explored the experiences, genetics, and early pre-verbal connections that form the blueprint of our lives. These issues increase our vulnerability to developing certain mental and physical health issues while our attachment style and parenting experiences determine how we view our self-worth, capabilities, and trust in others and the world. These factors greatly set the stage of our lives but are unknown to us as we develop through childhood and beyond.

Part II of the book discusses the experiences and events that dramatically affect who we are by shaping us throughout our lives. We will begin with trauma and psychological distress, expand to family dynamics and legacies, explore grief and loss, before ending with the impact of issues such as chronic mental illness and pain.

Chapter 4

Trauma and Psychological Distress

'People often say that this or that person has not yet found himself. But the self is not something one finds, it is something one creates.'

—Thomas Szasz

This chapter focuses on the impact of trauma over a lifetime. We will attempt to understand trauma in terms of how certain events overwhelm one's capacity to make memories and face certain knowledge and emotions, instead forming folders and subfolders to keep the fragments of memories, distressing knowledge and experiences, and pain at bay. While this works for a while, avoidance, denial, and other defence mechanisms meant to keep distressing knowledge out of our consciousness are temporary solutions. Overusing them leads to clients coming to therapy in distress because they feel dissociated, disconnected, and unable to find fulfilment in their lives and relationships.

The great shame, false narratives, and amount of self-knowledge buried under traumatic experiences is staggering. What individuals connect to instead is the sense of guilt, responsibility, and the confusion about why their lives and relationships feel broken. This chapter aims to help readers understand that dissociation and compartmentalization are not necessary. People are strong enough to command the knowledge and emotions buried within them and can come to fully accept themselves.

Trauma is defined as a severe and lasting emotional shock and pain caused by an extremely terrifying or upsetting experience.[76] In its purest definition, trauma has been thought of as the experience of a life threatening or altering event.

The common types of trauma are child abuse, sexual assault, discrimination, bullying, IPV, sex trafficking, natural disasters, war, religious persecution, community violence, traumatic grief, and medical trauma.[77] As you can imagine, this list is not exhaustive, and what one person finds traumatic may not apply to another.

Meanwhile, the diagnostic manual used by psychologists, the *Diagnostic and Statistical Manual of Mental Disorders* (DSM-V) identifies a traumatic event as exposure to threatened death, serious injury, or sexual violence. Such exposure may occur directly or indirectly by witnessing the event, learning the traumatic event occurred to a loved one, or repeated exposure to traumatic details of an event, like in the case of paramedics or police officers responding to emergency calls.[78]

Over 70 per cent of individuals worldwide report having experienced at least one traumatic event in their lifetime, with 30.5 per cent experiencing more than four traumatic events.[79] The most common types of trauma are witnessing death or serious injury, the unexpected death of a loved one, being mugged, being in a life-threatening motor vehicle accident, and experiencing a life-threatening illness or injury. These account for over 50 per cent of the traumatic events experienced by people.[80]

The types of traumatic events most commonly experienced as well as the average number of people experiencing that event varies by country, with significant differences between developed and undeveloped countries. For example, in developed countries, the percentage of individuals who have experienced at least one traumatic event actually vary between 28 to 90 per cent of individuals and the most common traumas experienced are the unexpected loss of a loved one, motor vehicle accidents, and muggings. The trauma of seeing deaths or meeting with accidents or being injured are more common in countries classified as low to middle income as opposed to high income ones.[81]

Gender differences have also been found in the forms of trauma experienced. Women experience more sexual assaults and IPV than men while men face more injuries, accidents, and physical assaults than women. As we have seen in previous chapters, early childhood trauma, like sexual or physical abuse or witnessing IPV, raises a person's likelihood of experiencing violence and being in abusive relationships later in life. Thus, individuals falling in this category are more likely to experience revictimization by experiencing a second or more traumatic event later in life.

Childhood Trauma

Trauma is a field that has been extensively researched but that we still continue to learn more about at a substantial rate. Due to the length of time for which trauma has been studied, we have been able to follow children who were abused at young ages and their parents to get a more complete understanding of the long-term effects of trauma on a developing child. As discussed in previous chapters, intergenerational trauma impacts the genes of a child even before they are born. We also know that traumatic experiences alter a child's mental and physical health, impacting how they engage with the world.

Those who have experienced childhood abuse have higher rates of mental issues—like PTSD, depression, disruptive behaviours, suicidality, substance use—and medical disorders—like cardiovascular disease, obesity, chronic pain syndromes, gastrointestinal disorders, and immune suppression.[82] In general, adults who have experienced childhood abuse struggle to maintain consistency at work, needing to take more time off and having higher rates of turnover. They also struggle to maintain relationships, with the existing ones being more chaotic, short lived, and violent. Although these facts can seem discouraging, it is important to keep in mind that they point to higher vulnerability and are not absolute. The majority of individuals experiencing childhood trauma are able to have secure, loving relationships, fulfilling lives, and successful careers. Furthermore, experiencing a consequence of childhood trauma is not the defining factor of someone's life. We need to uncover these vulnerabilities to create awareness and support in the form of early intervention and community education.

The psychological and physical impact of child abuse can be seen as early as the age of four or five through changes in behaviour. A child experiencing trauma or chronic stress during the first four years of their life impacts brain structures and systems that develop during that initial, critical time of life. A five-year-old experiencing trauma is three times more likely to have difficulty paying attention in class, and twice as likely to be aggressive.[83] Kids this age have trouble learning to read and write and have memory issues that impact their ability to learn new things. Experiencing trauma changes a child's brain because they live in a state of constant danger and crisis created by situations like child abuse and IPV. This is made worse if a child is constantly neglected or deprived of food and other such important resources.

A child who experiences trauma is often in fight or flight mode, with parts of the brain, like the amygdala, being in overdrive and signalling danger to the rest of the body. The hippocampus, another area of the brain associated with memory, being similarly affected explains problems in learning, especially learning new information. The prefrontal cortex—an area of the brain responsible for higher order thinking like impulsivity, decision making, information processing, concentration, and more—also being overwhelmed and impacted makes it less effective. Additionally, chronic stress leads to increased arousal of the hypothalamic–pituitary–adrenal axis (HPA axis), which can be thought of as the body's stress system. This dysregulation can continue into later years through the overstimulation or suppression of the stress hormone system. A child's body and brain are flooded by stress hormones at the expense of them being present and able to utilize their full cognitive functioning. Taken together, these changes in brain structure mean the child is often overstimulated and has difficulty regulating their emotional experience. A child in this state can appear overly active, aggressive, non-compliant, and irritable or subdued, zoned out, disconnected, and unresponsive. Both are responses to feeling overwhelmed with emotion, anxiety, and stress and come at the cost of learning, emotional development, and making and maintaining positive relationships.

Signs a Child Is Being Abused (for Parents and Guardians)

Under Five (Preschool)

- Bed wetting
- Nightmares
- Increased fear of separation from parents
- Changes in eating habits

Elementary School

In addition to the signs mentioned above, look out for:
- Refusing to go to school
- Acting out

- Irritability
- Aggressiveness
- Changes in grades
- Difficulty learning and retaining new information
- Problems with memory

Middle School and High School

In addition to the signs mentioned above, look out for:
- Drinking, smoking, or using substances
- Risky behaviours (like shoplifting, sexually risky behaviour)
- Withdrawal from parents
- Missing school
- Evidence of eating disorders (restricting food, excessive exercise, eating in private)
- Self-harm

Post-Traumatic Stress Disorder

When we think about trauma, PTSD often comes to mind. It is important to state that most individuals who experience a traumatic event do not develop PTSD. Studies conducted globally indicate that the prevalence of PTSD varies depending on the country. Some studies have found the prevalence of PTSD to be as low as 1.7 per cent of the population in a country like South Korea[84] and as high as 9.2 per cent in Canada.[85] A study in 2008 set out to study incidences of PTSD across twenty-six countries. The authors found that on average the global prevalence of PTSD was 3.9 per cent, with half of the individuals surveyed reporting persistent symptoms.[86]

A major barrier to finding accurate statistics is differences in reporting between high- and low-income countries. This could reflect differences in attitudes to mental illness, education and support available, and resources and opportunities to seek help. People in higher income countries were found to seek help almost twice as often (53.5 per cent) as those from lower income countries (23.7 per cent). This leads to more accurate numbers of PTSD diagnoses among higher income countries. Certain risk factors are related to developing PTSD, including socio-economic instability, lower household income, and being unmarried, young, female, less educated, and unemployed.[87]

Now that we have an understanding of the prevalence of PTSD, we can look at what it actually means. PTSD is a psychiatric disorder that individuals who have experienced or witnessed a traumatic event can develop. To meet the criteria for diagnosis, a person must persistently re-experience the trauma through intrusive thoughts, memories, nightmares, flashbacks, or through emotional distress or physiological reactions to reminders of the traumatic situation. Re-experiencing trauma in these ways tends to haunt the individual and makes them feel overwhelmed by it and helpless to prevent it.

Often, when re-experiencing traumatic events, a person loses their sense of time and place, feeling like they are reliving the trauma all over again. The experience can be completely disorienting. While some people may have little to no memory of the events, others might vividly remember the details.

In addition to the criteria stated above, a person must demonstrate avoidance of either trauma-related thoughts and feelings or reminders. In essence, people intensely react to triggering events, people, and stimuli associated with their traumas. They experience a natural and protective avoidance, which they may not be able to put into words.

Additionally, following the traumatic event, people must display at least two of the following symptoms: difficulty recalling key elements of the trauma, overly negative thoughts and assumptions about oneself or the world, exaggeratedly blaming oneself or others for causing the trauma, negative emotions, decreased interest in activities, feeling isolated, or difficulty experiencing positive emotions.

Lastly, people must experience at least two of the following arousal related issues: irritability or aggression, risky or destructive behaviour, hypervigilance, pronounced startle reaction, difficulty concentrating, difficulty sleeping.[88]

In order to qualify as a diagnosis, symptoms have to last for more than a month and be influential enough to interfere with people's functioning by, for instance, impairing their social or occupational lives.

As you can see PTSD encompasses a wide array of symptoms, many of which we can see in children and adults who have experienced trauma. However, to be diagnosed with PTSD, people must meet some specific criteria, including having numerous of these symptoms.

The *Diagnostic and Statistical Manual of Mental Disorders, 5th edition* (DSM-V, 2013) includes a related subtype of PTSD for children under six. The re-experiencing of trauma does not have to be distressing for children that young. In fact, some children can appear more bright or neutral. In addition, the threshold for children in terms of avoidance and changes in mood is lower.

Let's take the example of Elias. He's a five-year-old boy who was brought to therapy by his mother. Just eight months earlier, Elias had lost his father to a motorcycle accident. Between the age of three and five, children usually understand what death is. By the age of five, they more or less understand that death is irreversible, and that dead people never come back. Elias was four when his father passed away.

Elias' mom was young and overwhelmed with her own grief. She had another child who was only a year old. She thought Elias had been coping and starting to feel better about the loss of his father. He was playing with friends, going to school. She heard him laugh, saw him smile. The initial couple of months of the loss had been devastating for both of them, but she had seen glimpses of hope that her son was getting better. What she did not know was that while she was grappling with the grief of losing her husband, her son had experienced it as a major traumatic event.

She started to realize something was wrong when she could not reconcile his often-cheery demeanour with some of the things his teachers were saying about him. He was often spacey in class, with his teachers having to call his name often. When he responded, he was bright and cooperative but always seemed to take a while to remember where he was and what he was doing. He grew very upset when he answered incorrectly, took too long to do something, or felt like he was not listening and misbehaving. When his teachers tried to talk to him about his father, Elias always said he missed him but seemed quite nonchalant while speaking about him and his passing. In fact, they had turned down school counselling because Elias said he did not want to meet anyone, and his teachers did not have any concrete reason to push him at that time.

Then, for a month before bringing him to therapy, Elias' mom had grown increasingly concerned because he had started talking about nightmares and seeing a 'devil' who hurt his father. When he first began speaking about the creature he was seeing, he did not find it threatening. However, it soon came to be more nefarious when Elias started saying that the creature asked him to do things. One of these things was to light paper on fire. Elias' mom was understandably worried and brought him in when he started expressing fear of the creature. Elias started feeling terrified of seeing images of his father being hurt by this devil who was keeping him from them. He started to feel even more scared that the devil would hurt him, his mother, or sister too.

At school, he often said cruel things he had never before and was physically aggressive more often. On the nights his mother could get him to his bed, he started wetting the bed. On other nights, he clung to her and refused to leave her bed. Elias' mom did not understand what was happening. This was not how she pictured her son experiencing grief. She worried that he was developing something like schizophrenia or that he would hurt himself or someone else.

When Elias finally overcame his fear of speaking about this 'devil', we understood what it symbolized to him. He had internalized the concept of a devil being responsible for the bad things that happened to his father to make sense of them. Elias did not have a real understanding of the dangers that came with riding a motorcycle or how this could have happened to his father. Motorcycles were something for which his father and him had a shared love. It was their hobby. They played games with it and washed it on the weekends. Elias idolized his father and could not wait till the day he would be allowed to ride his father's motorcycle with him.

Elias' family were religious and often went to church. He had a strong sense that the devil was responsible for evil in the world and had latched onto that concept. In school and at home, he felt worried about making mistakes or being uncooperative because of his fear of being punished by this devil for not being good. His world had turned upside down with the loss of his father and, in doing so, had changed his view of the world. What he had taken for granted as a safe world through his childhood naivete had become fragile and overwhelming in its uncertainty. He was terrified that he would lose his mother or sister every time they walked out of the door. Even more so, he was worried that him misbehaving would cause their deaths. Like many people who have experienced the trauma of losing someone violently, the biggest price Elias paid was losing his sense of safety and trust in the world.

Elias was able to understand there was no 'devil' during the course of his therapy. He realized that what he experienced through his nightmares and intrusive thoughts were actually his buried fear, anger, and confusion. His aggression and irritability were symptoms of his trauma and reflected the anger he felt about the loss of his father but could not express. Elias was able to learn how to regulate his emotions, understand his fears, and begin the process of living without his father. Although Elias experienced quite a few symptoms of PTSD, it is important to note that he was not diagnosed with PTSD and stopped having its symptoms with the help and support of his family and therapy. He still misses his father but can continue therapy to keep himself from burying his love and connection with his father. Instead, he is learning to honour his father's presence and role as he grows into a pre-teen.

Elias is an example of the devastating impact of trauma, and how important it is for family and teachers to learn its signs. They are not always as evident as one might think, and children can present their difficulties under the guise of recovering, even cheeriness. We need to know these signs because PTSD or not, therapy helps a child deal with the issue instead of burying it, unprocessed. They learn to cope with the difficult emotions and urges by acting in ways that are unlike them.

If denied the opportunity to heal, children often bring the loss of a parent into their later relationships, acting out their unresolved trauma and fears. Frequently, adults with unprocessed trauma find it difficult to be emotionally vulnerable and forthcoming with their partners. This often leads to difficulties with emotional intimacy and trust in their later relationship, which can sometimes be brought to light in couples therapy. Given the right support, children are very resilient and can overcome most things. More children by far will overcome the impact of a trauma they have experienced than those who will struggle with their trauma over a lifetime.

The Immune System and Childhood Trauma

Prolonged chronic stress, particularly PTSD, can have a long-term impact on the immune system. These changes to the immune system can lead to increased risk of autoimmune diseases and inflammation markers.[89] Autoimmune disorders commonly related to PTSD are irritable bowel syndrome (IBS), multiple sclerosis (MS), psoriasis, rheumatoid arthritis, lupus, and more.[90] Physical illnesses associated with PTSD include asthma, cardiovascular diseases, cardiovascular events like heart failure and ischemia, and type II diabetes.[91]

The exact relationship between PTSD and immune system issues, like autoimmune disorders, is still being explored. Research points to increased inflammation causing autoimmune disorders.[92] However, it has also been explored if there are any immune or inflammation related vulnerabilities among individuals who experience a traumatic event and then go on to develop PTSD.[93] Furthermore, disrupted sleep patterns, increased substance use, and the high level of stress associated with PTSD also account for an unknown portion of the increased inflammation, risk of developing physical illnesses, and immune system dysregulation.

To better understand the impact of trauma and chronic stress on an individual's immune system and physical health, let us look at Katie. She was twenty-one when she came to therapy and had a long history of verbal abuse and neglect by her parents. She had also been sexually abused by her uncle—her mother's brother. Her relationship with her mother was highly stressful and full of conflict. It was made worse by the fact that her mother did not believe her brother had hurt Katie. Katie's mother dismissed her allegations, changing the subject and shutting her down when she spoke about it.

Katie oscillated between trying to set boundaries and get space from her mother and trying to get her to be the mother she needed. While she struggled with the impact of what her uncle had done, she felt even more betrayed that her mother did not believe her. She needed her mother to believe her because she already felt a constant sense of shame and believed that she was deeply unlovable after what had happened to her. She had told no one other than her mother. After her mother accused her of making things up, she was even more determined to never share it with anyone. She often felt conflicted about her mother, to the point of struggling to sleep or concentrate and feeling strongly pained about it. She also felt angry at her mother. She had an ever-growing inkling that her mother should have believed her. Her buried intuition told her that she had not done anything wrong and that she was actually the one who had been wronged by the adults in her life who had failed to protect her.

She started therapy with this inkling, beginning to realize the impact of the constant stress of her relationship with her parents and a long-buried trauma that had shaped her confidence in herself and others since she had been a child. At the start of therapy, Katie had a difficult time functioning. She was aware of the issues with her parents and remembered the abuse from her past. However, she came because she could not bear her constant anxiety and suspected it had someone to do with her frequent illnesses. Katie had been experiencing everything from recurrent ulcers to gastric issues, getting sick almost every month. Not too long ago, she had started feeling constantly fatigued, her joints aching, always feeling like she was on the verge of having a cold. At just twenty-one, she felt like a woman twice her age. This rocked her fragile sense of confidence even more and caused her to spend more time at home.

The more time she was at home, the less she saw her friends or took part in the activities like boxing that quelled her anxiety. Her parents had little patience for her frequent illnesses. They accused her of seeking attention, whining, and made comments that she would forever freeload off them because she would never be able to have a job or her own apartment. Katie felt entirely responsible for bringing these issues on herself and thought that she deserved her family's comments.

In reality, Katie was proactive about seeking help, she frequently went to her primary care physician to get answers and was soon taking an array of supplements to build her immunity. She felt discouraged by the lack of answers and defeated because of the feeling that her body was slowly breaking down. This sense of helplessness and hopelessness surrounding her health only furthered her anxiety and depression, depleting her confidence.

In addition, Katie had started displaying symptoms of an eating disorder, restricting her food intake and the types of food she ate. Initially, this had been an effort to rule out allergies and identify the role of food in creating inflammation in her body. However, it became apparent that the level of control she sought over her body was further hurting her. Katie felt like her eating was the only thing she could control in a chaotic home and body she felt she was losing ownership over.

Her therapy progressed slowly. Many of the issues that brought her to therapy were also protective strategies she used to cope with the world. Working on one issue such as the eating disorder started impacting her level of anxiety. Working on setting boundaries in her relationship with her parents caused her to restrict her food intake further, and she struggled to sleep.

We slowly began to uncover how the stress and hyperarousal she was experiencing because of her PTSD were connected to her physical health. She began to notice that periods of sickness seemed to follow periods of depression and heightened PTSD symptoms. This helped us to realize that Katie was experiencing recurrent illnesses because of her mental health issues and the chronic high stress she experienced at home. She was able to approach her health in a more proactive and targeted way, leading her to an autoimmune specialist. Katie was diagnosed with lupus. Although she had a tough journey ahead of her, receiving adequate treatment allowed her to feel more empowered. She started to change her lifestyle and habits, which led to improvements in her overall health. She also learned to manage her stress when experiencing a flare up.

Over time, Katie's quality of life drastically improved as she started to get her lupus symptoms under control, understand her PTSD and anxiety, and resolve the buried feelings of rejection, being unlovable, and shame she felt because of her childhood abuse and relationship with her parents. Moving out of her house and into an apartment with roommates who respected her space was a significant milestone for her. I will not say that she did not struggle, but she finally understood that her PTSD did not operate in a vacuum. She learned to recognize early signs of both her autoimmune disorder, the impact of her parents on her mental landscape, and how to gain perspective of the issues that affected her mental health.

The benefit of knowing there is a link between PTSD and autoimmune disorders is that we can make plans for early intervention with anti-inflammatory treatments. This is especially important because autoimmune disorders and inflammation can be hard to diagnose and the path to treatment and relief can often be a long and drawn-out process while someone suffers.

Risk and Protective Factors of Trauma and Related Disorders

To intervene early, we need to understand who is at risk. The strongest vulnerability factor is previous exposure to a traumatic event like childhood abuse, witnessing IPV, experiencing a traumatic death, or a complicated and traumatizing medical illness. There are several theories behind why the aforementioned factors increase the risk of experiencing trauma and related disorders—links have been found to increased psychological vulnerability in the form of low self-esteem and feeling powerless. Other theories point to increased risky behaviours and lowered ability to manage dangerous or risky situations as explanations.

Similarly, certain factors increase people's vulnerability to trauma and decrease their capability to handle it. These factors are largely related to their families and communities. Overall, the stability of people's families impacts how they deal with trauma. Specific risk factors such as an adverse childhood environment, childhood neglect, level of life stress pre-trauma, and maltreatment in family have been found to be most connected to developing traumatic reactions or PTSD.[94]

If you think about it, family, community, and school build the foundation of a child's life. A child who grows up in a chaotic or neglectful household can miss out on building a connection with individuals who can help them make sense of their experiences, guide them through their stressors and problems, and provide the stability to move past issues.

Families with less education or income in which someone is ill, disabled, incarcerated, or which struggle to make ends meet were found to be at increased risk. Likewise, a family's way of communicating (i.e., aggressive, hostile), views of violence, use of physical punishment for discipline, and the extent of conflict in it can also be risk factors. Similarly, the community an individual lives in can be protective or act as a risk factor. Communities with more violence and access to drugs, higher unemployment rates, poverty, and low social resources are a risk. Additionally, low community cohesion, transient communities with people frequently moving and less community opportunities for younger individuals make a significant difference. A good way to think about it is that an individual's community and school can act as a buffer for neglect or chaos at home by providing stability and avenues for seeking support. Instead of feeling isolated and deprived, community opportunities provide a hopeful path forward.

The severity of the trauma itself is not associated with higher adverse reactions and PTSD. Instead, it is the person's subjective experience of the trauma. The perceived threat to life is particularly linked to PTSD. I have met many individuals who have come to therapy and been adamant that they do not want to discuss something 'traumatic' from their past, which they have moved past or do not believe impacts them. This is often the case with assault, sexual abuse, or loss. In some cases, the person has never faced the trauma and is worried about unearthing something painful that will hurt them more. Often though, the individual is correct, and they either never viewed the event as traumatic or processed and moved on from it without developing any adverse reactions. The goal of therapy is never to make what could seem like an objectively traumatizing event a focus of therapy when the client is there for other reasons. The client is, after all, the expert of their own experience.

Among those who develop PTSD, higher levels of psychopathology, depression, and life stress are usually more common in the year leading up to the traumatic event, which prompt the PTSD. For example, if someone is experiencing an anxiety or depressive disorder then their thinking about the trauma can be distorted to imagine the worst case scenarios. They underestimate themselves and feel more helpless about overcoming their trauma. Due to the propensity of anxiety to be tangled with intrusive thoughts and ruminative thinking, such people are more likely to re-experience the trauma and feel more frequent distress. This pattern is akin to depression, which evokes similar negative feelings about the past, oneself, and the future, leaving people feeling more hopeless and helpless. Depression also causes distorted thinking, which can lead to people catastrophizing and finding it difficult to move past the traumatic incident.

Social support can be both a risk and a protective factor for most mental health issues and recovery from them. People with support from friends and family are more likely to seek professional help and have opportunities to discuss and process their experiences. Furthermore, the support of others allows inaccurate thoughts and beliefs around the trauma to be challenged. For example, someone may believe that no one will want to be with them after an assault or that they played a role in causing the trauma. A friend or relative has enough distance from the situation to be able to tell the person that these thoughts are a product of the trauma and encourage them to seek help if things worsen. On the other hand, social constraints or the lack of social support can leave people isolated and increase feelings of alienation and otherness stemming from trauma. Additionally, social constraints can discourage people from seeking help or legal action, exacerbate their stigma, and contribute to victim blaming. This can stop them from seeking help and, worse, lead to them developing flawed beliefs, including self-blame and shame.

Other protective factors increase people's resilience to trauma and stop them from reaching adverse outcomes. While discussing risk factors, it is important to keep in mind that children are resilient and overcome trauma and chaotic upbringings every day. Protective factors that build resilience are just as powerful at moderating people's ability to overcome. Protective factors found to be the most helpful are related to social support and stability. A family that provides for a child's needs, supervises appropriately, and creates an environment of nurturing, positive connection, and support promotes resilience and moderates against the impact of trauma. Families that provide a model for handling difficult emotions and solving conflict peacefully and give children a safe space to talk about their issues go a long way in helping children navigate trauma and manage difficult moments. The good news is, research has proved that, for children, having at least one loving and stable adult who provides consistent support greatly buffers and makes up for lack of support received otherwise.[95]

A higher education level and greater 'cognitive capacity' are also protective factors against developing PTSD.[96] They protect both the child and parent, as greater flexibility and knowledge allow individuals to better solve problems, gain perspectives, and approach life's struggles with an opportunistic approach. Likewise, a supportive and welcoming neighbourhood or immediate community is another protective factor. Finally, access to safe and nurturing childcare, quality education, and individuals within these systems aiming to help families and their children at a social, emotional, and academic level make a difference. These systems offer hope and encouragement and facilitate identifiable avenues of progress and opportunity.

This is important information to keep in mind. It can be easy to feel weighed down by circumstances out of your control. Am

I home enough for my child? Do I work enough and provide enough? What happens if I get divorced? None of us can have perfect families or be and do everything. The most helpful thing you can do is provide the most stable environment you can and let your child know you are there for them, emotionally and physically. If one is struggling, connecting to communities that offer more social and economic support can make all the difference. Children are resilient, they can and will overcome the struggles parents face if you can create awareness, openness, and a desire to work through one's circumstances.

Trauma and Dissociation

Dissociation is a lesser-known response to trauma. Although, it is known in the mental health discourse as central to trauma reactions. According to the DSM-V, dissociation is defined as a disruption or disconnect from behaviour, memory, consciousness, emotion, perception, or in some cases, identity.[97] It is helpful to think of dissociation as a continuum. We all dissociate to some degree, most often in a normal, healthy manner. For example, if you are driving on autopilot and suddenly realize you are nearly home then you have experienced a disruption in conscious awareness. Daydreaming or getting lost in a book are all mild forms of dissociation that most people experience.

On the end of the spectrum are those who have disconnected from aspects of their identity to the extent of having several distinct personalities. This is called dissociative identity disorder (DID). Those who experience more than mild dissociation often have experienced trauma, particularly prolonged, chronic childhood abuse, or adversity. It is helpful to think of dissociation as a creative coping strategy that people use when they feel mentally overwhelmed or are met with a situation they cannot escape or solve. This can happen in several ways. During a traumatic event, people often dissociate in a way to separate themselves from the trauma. For example, when people are being assaulted, they may check out, not consciously process information, and, as a result, may struggle to put together the details of that event. Often, their memories are patchy, and they can feel confused about whether certain things happened.

This particularly happens in situations of chronic abuse. For example, a child who is being sexually abused may escape in their minds to another place where the abuse is not happening. Between assaults, that child may disconnect from the negative emotions, fear, or the felt presence of abuse, allowing them to function. In these situations, the child may appear bright and cheerful and, when necessary, maintain a functional relationship with their abuser.

Similarly, individuals who have been assaulted have described out of body experiences, where they feel as if they are viewing themselves from above or outside their bodies instead of experiencing the assault. This can also be described as similar to watching a movie or seeing things through a tunnel. If you think about it, this is a creative way for the mind to not absorb the full impact of the horrors it is experiencing.

Dissociation can become problematic when people begin to use it as their primary coping strategy. Initially, individuals dissociate in response to danger and threats. But, over time, they start dissociating increasingly indiscriminately—during difficult conversations, when feeling strong emotions, or even facing everyday problems.

The problem with dissociation is that it tends to linger for a while, sometimes days, making the person feel foggy, disconnected, and often losing time. People describe these periods of dissociation as unpleasant because they struggle to motivate themselves, concentrate, or accomplish the things they need to. It is often a very isolated process, with people finding it hard to be around others and even harder to connect when they are surrounded by people. In this sense, dissociation can be a trigger for self-harm and substance use, as people struggle to ground themselves and feel something.

The other part of dissociation that can be disturbing involves memory loss. Dissociation can create a disconnect in individuals' memories. This tends to happen in severe cases of dissociation, when individuals are experiencing the traumatic event itself, or among people who have certain dissociative disorders. This dissociative amnesia can last mere minutes or for years. Sometimes, people may be missing the years in which the trauma occurred, which is especially likely in the case of chronic childhood trauma because of which adults may miss certain portions of their childhood. Other times, they may have spotty memories and feel spacey, forgetting important conversations, whole days, and important events. In the latter situations, people can wonder if there is something wrong with their brains. This form of amnesia feels different from the way people normally forget things, which feels particularly scary. It is important to note that this information does not simply disappear but is, instead, repressed, akin to being stored in folders and subfolders, any of which can impact a person greatly if triggered to open. If a 'folder' does open, people can feel scared and disoriented, as they are not consciously aware of its contents. Furthermore, individuals can have trouble trusting themselves or their sense of identity, as the sense of continuity in their memories is disrupted, making it difficult to discern between reality and fantasy or dream.

There are different types of dissociation, such as depersonalization and derealization. One of the most commonly experienced forms—depersonalization—is a type of dissociative experience that can occur in response to trauma and, often, anxiety or a panic attack. People experiencing depersonalization feel disconnected from themselves or their bodies. It feels like they are not real or are distorted. This can also apply to certain body parts.

Derealization, on the other hand, is the sense that the world or environment around are not real or have changed in some way.

Sometimes, people describe feeling as though they are watching a movie of what is happening instead of living it. Both experiences are not something to be overly concerned about although they can feel extremely disconcerting when they occur. Usually, derealization and depersonalization pass quite quickly, even though overall dissociation may linger.

One last thing to take note of about dissociation is that it can disrupt people's sense of identity and self. There are several types of dissociative disorders outlined in the DSM-V, which are dissociative identity disorder, depersonalization/derealization disorder, dissociative amnesia (including dissociative fugue), other specified dissociative disorder, and unspecified dissociative disorder. What these dissociative disorders have in common at their core are memory disturbances, derealization, depersonalization, and alteration of and confusion regarding one's identity. Unfortunately, dissociative disorders are often underdiagnosed and frequently overlooked. In fact, it has been found to take someone with a dissociative disorder an average of 5 to 12.4 years of active participation in treatment before getting an accurate diagnosis.[98] This is highly unfortunate, as people experiencing dissociation often feel like they are losing their minds or have something seriously wrong with them before they understand which of their symptoms can be attributed to dissociation. Additionally, the delayed diagnosis and misdiagnosis of dissociative disorders is costly to both individuals and their communities. It has been argued that accurate diagnosis leads to a 25–64 per cent reduction in healthcare utilization and costs.[99] Most importantly, early diagnosis can reduce the severity of patients' distress and symptoms.

As many as 60 per cent of individuals with dissociative disorders consider themselves unable to work due to the severity of symptoms. Nevertheless, the most serious of these dissociative disorders is dissociative identity disorder (DID). It is a relatively rare (although much less rare than the public thinks) disorder that afflicts about 1.9 per cent of the global population.[100] It is hard to get accurate statistics about dissociative disorders in general but particularly DID. Numbers are underreported, treatment is inconsistent, and misdiagnosis happens at a higher rate than most other mental health disorders.

In the past, you may have heard of DID being referred to as multiple personality disorder. This diagnosis has been inaccurately sensationalized due to movies like *Identity*, *Split*, and *Sybil*. People have been fascinated by the movie version of DID, which depicts individuals with distinct people living inside them. Each 'personality' is exaggerated in the media to have their own individual lives unknown to the central identity, and there is often at least one personality with malicious or sinister intentions. In reality, DID involves two or more distinct identities or states of personality. Each personality state is fairly distinct and has its own way of perceiving, interacting, and thinking about themselves, others, and their environments.

DID and dissociation in general, really, are examples of the impact burying memories, emotions, experiences, behaviours, and more can have on a person's ability to live a functioning and fulfilling life. More than 90 per cent of those diagnosed with DID have a history of childhood trauma, particularly chronic or severe trauma. Effectively, a person takes unacceptable emotions, fears, experiences, and behaviours and project them onto another identity or part of themselves. The part or identity holds a purpose for the person and allows them to function in a less hindered way. Having parts that hold difficult experiences protects them in different ways, allowing them to be the child or person they want to be in their present life. For example, a person may have a four-year-old part who holds all of the trauma, fear, doubts, and damage they experienced at that age. The part may be a distinct personality, acting like a four-year-old, engaging in play and childish behaviour and thoughts or be less defined, holding emotions and the trauma but no sense of identity. That same person may have an abuser part who was formed to help the child cope with abuse but now damages the person more by abusing the self. Often, the abuser part is created so the child can maintain their attachment and relationship with a parent, family member, or caregiver who is abusive. This part holds difficult memories, emotions, and thoughts about the real abuser and allows the child to continue to love and feel positively about the abuser.

Not all parts of a person with DID are created at once. Some parts may be created over the course of their lives as needed. For example, a part may be created when the person is a teenager who is social, likable, and fun. This allows the person to separate their experiences of neglect and abuse and feel accepted and liked by peers.

Most of the people I have met and worked with who have DID are extremely bright and creative individuals. It takes a remarkable mind and strength to create a system to protect someone from some of the horrors children can experience at the hands of others. One client I had the opportunity to work with was a testament to the power of the mind's ability to protect and shield us from situations we cannot handle face on.

Let us look at Briana's case, for example. When she first came to me, she was a woman in her fifties who had faced incredible and horrific trauma as a child into her adult years. It took nearly a year of therapy to understand the extent and nature of the trauma she had experienced, as it was held and protected savagely by her identities. Her central identity was a funny, smart, and heavily guarded woman. Meeting her meant passing her tests to see if she could begin to trust you. Any hint that you could not handle her or that she was too much for a person would lead to her swiftly shuttering up and never returning.

Brianna, luckily, had been to therapists before and was aware of at least some of her alter identities. She was able to, at most times, control them from taking over her consciousness and could remain consciously aware when another identity took over.

Brianna had a five-year-old identity, which held the worst of the abuse. She had grown up in an impoverished family that could pay little attention to her, as they focused on their own financial and economic instability as well as the depression and anxiety that permeated her family on both sides. As a result, Brianna was mostly left to her own devices, which is how she preferred it. Her dad was quick to anger and became unpredictable. She had a difficult time being around her mother when she was drinking.

Brianna had spent a lot of time with her neighbours and extended family, which felt like enough for her. Plus, she rationalized that she loved her parents dearly and they had good times together when they were not so stressed. The primary trouble began when Brianna started being groomed and eventually sexually abused by an older cousin. Brianna's aunt and her three boys were a big part of her life. She did not know how to think about her abuse. She knew that her cousin was beloved by her mother and her aunt. She also knew, on some level, that what was happening was not right. Not knowing who to turn to or what to make of the confusing actions of the cousin she loved, Brianna mentally escaped to magical lands she created in vivid detail. She did not hold on to the details of the abuse because she was dissociating.

When her cousin had gone to college, the abuse stopped but Brianna did not register the change. She continued to live as she had, not knowing how to protect herself or what signs she should look out for to know when an adult meant to hurt her.

As we've discussed, experiencing one traumatic event makes a person more susceptible to experiencing another. She had gone on to be abused by a neighbour and later a partner. Some of the trauma caught up with Brianna in her teen years when she had difficulty knowing how to have regular, age-appropriate friendships. Even worse, boys in her school were starting to show interest in her, and she did not share the same level of excitement or interest in them as the girls around her. She started to feel abnormal, like something was wrong with her. She felt that she was not in on the secret to fitting in and belonging, which her peers all seemed to naturally know. She had begun to recognize that her home life was not the same as many of her friends. She did not like to have people over because of her parent's unpredictable behaviours and the neglect she experienced in her household. She was embarrassed and increasingly angry at her situation and family.

Sometimes, she would lose track of time when she got overwhelmed with emotions. Other times, she would become disproportionately angry and lash out at people at school. These were the times her five-year-old and abuser parts were beginning to slip into her consciousness. Around this time, Brianna's friends had also started to comment on the changes in her behaviour. They would come up to her and ask her why she was so lively, social, and gregarious at times and, at other times, it was like she barely knew what to say to them. She was reserved, guarded, and wanted little to do with them. Brianna was very confused by these statements and shrugged them off for the most part of her teens and twenties. It was not till she was in her thirties that Brianna began to understand her experiences, like gaps of time, forgotten conversations and events, or even finding clothes she did not remember buying. People with DID have experiences like these, including coming across individuals who they do not recognize calling them names, being accused of lying about things they have no memory of, and acting distinctly out of character for their central identity. Brianna had accepted that she had a poor memory and considered herself spacey and forgetful. However, the things she had been experiencing were far past normal forgetfulness.

Brianna had been experiencing and developing other identities since she was five years old. She had little awareness of this when she started therapy in her thirties or forties. All of this had been buried. What she did experience were panic attacks, depression, suicidal thoughts, and episodes of self-harm. She did not realize at that time that these were symptoms of severe dissociation, to the point of her not being able to function. For example, she would self-harm when she dissociated to the point of feeling cut off and numb about her emotions, including happiness and sadness, and connection to others. She felt as though self-harm made her feel something, and the pain was better than numbness. The depression came on with intrusive feelings of low self-worth and shame around her body, although she did not know why. Worse, the depression made her dissociate more and she felt like she would lose track of her days during this time. In fact, when she was more depressed or overwhelmed about things like school and friends, her identities would take over more easily as she resisted less and, in some ways, welcomed the break from reality.

People with DID often show this pattern and deal with stress by disappearing for a few days or more. Dissociating makes room for more 'competent' alter identities to take control of the situation. For example, one of Brianna's teenage identities would come to the forefront to fit in and connect with others when Brianna lacked the confidence to do so. This would be the case when her friends would perceive her as outgoing and talkative. She also developed an alter who was confident and flirty with boys but not weighed down by the knowledge of her childhood abuse.

People usually do not feel much control over their identities in the beginning. This is a larger issue because while a diagnosis requires at least two identities, some studies estimate that, on average, a person can have up to sixteen identities by adulthood.[101] Identities can also integrate and disappear over time and do so at a faster rate during treatment.

The problem for many people, like Brianna, is that it is difficult to break out of a dissociative episode when they are not doing well mentally and emotionally, as is usually the case during a dissociative episode.

Brianna had to see a few therapists before being correctly diagnosed with DID (it can take an average of six therapists to reach a correct diagnosis of a dissociative disorder). She was afraid at first but slowly began to realize the protective purposes of her identities. Brianna had about fifteen identities she knew of when she started her treatment with me in her early fifties.

The goal of treatment with DID is co-consciousness and integration. Essentially, we want the individual to be in the driver's seat at all times but learn to listen and learn from other parts of their identity. Picture a boardroom where decisions can be made by all parts and moderated by the main identity. All parts hold information like disconnected memories, emotion, knowledge, and patterns of thinking, which the main identity benefits from knowing. Learning to look at it as a collaboration instead of a fight for power or dominance helps the individual feel less afraid and overwhelmed.

Brianna, over time, was able to incorporate some of her identities that were less well formed and essential to her functioning during her first round of therapy. In her fifties, she was accepting that she had to let go of and integrate some of her central identities, such as the five-year-old and abuser personality. While she wanted to overcome her abuser identity, she was very afraid of the vulnerability that would come without the protection of this personality and feared what embracing the emotions carried by that identity would do to her relationships with those who had abused or neglected her during her childhood.

Treatment was largely focused on dealing with the resistance around this issue and, to a great extent, the resistance and emotions the alter identities experienced at the threat of merging. Among most DID patients, the most effective treatment happens when they have a solid and trustworthy relationship with their therapists. Then, they are able to explore all buried and compartmentalized fears, traumas, emotions, and experiences. Over time, Brianna and her other identities were able to agree that integration preserved them all and made them stronger together. In order to get this point, Brianna had to face the trauma and truths buried in each identity. She was rightfully scared and confronting that which each part had to share was a slow and painful journey. During this time, Brianna would often dissociate and not come to therapy and help herself. This happened even more so when more unhelpful identities surfaced and resisted exposing Brianna to her buried truths. Despite these challenges, Brianna, with the help of other parts of her identity, managed to achieve co-consciousness and continued to take strides toward full integration.

The Impact of Trauma on the Self

Like dissociation, trauma can change how people think about themselves and bury the whole and accurate truth of their situations. Unfortunately, people's first natural response to trauma tends to be a sense of shame coupled with questioning their role and responsibility in bringing about the trauma. This is especially the case in situations like sexual assault in which society questions the moral character and actions of the victims, leading to cultures of internalized victim blaming and shaming. When experiencing a traumatic event, a person can struggle to comprehend and process what is happening. As discussed, dissociation and compartmentalization play a large role in protecting a person from experiencing the full pain and horror of a traumatic event. This also makes it more difficult for the person to know what really happened and access their emotions and memories around the event.

In fact, when people start to think about a traumatic event, they often slip into experiencing a level of dissociation similar to one they experienced during the event. They may feel that the traumatic event happened to someone else or that they were not present when it occurred. This shakes such people's confidence in their memory and version of events, particularly when thinking about disclosing their trauma to someone else. This is why it is common for individuals who have experienced certain traumatic events (like sexual assault and childhood abuse) to hold off on disclosing them for many years. During that time, they also abstain from fully acknowledging these traumas to themselves or they may acknowledge the trauma to themselves but choose not to disclose it for several reasons.

In the first case, a person may not have fully acknowledged the trauma. They may be too overwhelmed by the situation and feel incapable of handling it. This is especially the case if the person is still experiencing the trauma or is still connected to the abuser. Take, for example, Joy. She was a seventeen-year-old who came to therapy for anxiety and suspected ADHD. She lived with her father and younger brother. Her parents had separated after a highly contentious divorce seven years ago, which included allegations of abuse against Joy's father. Joy had not spoken to her mother for over a year, after several years of feeling torn between both households. Joy felt responsible for her younger brother. She also had a younger sister, who had ended up living with her mother, and she missed her sister greatly. The divorce and what ensued had torn them part emotionally, with each child feeling forced to choose sides. Unfortunately, choosing sides meant complete alienation from the other parent and siblings. Joy already felt like she had failed her youngest sister by allowing her to believe her mother's distorted view of her father and the events that led to their divorce. Joy took on the parentified role of protecting her younger siblings from the conflict and aggression she had witnessed. Once Joy made the choice to side with her father and stay with her younger brother, she felt there was no turning back. While she missed her mother at first, over time, she felt her resolve solidify that her mother was the problem here. She had tried to remain on her mother's good side to be able to see her youngest sister, but, over time, she could not bear the conflict and chaos it caused. Every visit to her mother was preceded and followed by questions and anger on both sides. Each visit was used by her parents for leverage and power over the other. After one particularly bad visit, Joy and her brother stopped going over, which led to a blow up with their mother, who ceased all contact.

Joy decided that her father had been right about her mother all along. How could she believe her mother when she could so easily cut her and her brother off? How could she try to turn them against her father in such a vicious and manipulative way? Joy threw herself into looking after her younger brother. She did not notice that she slowly had begun to take the role of a parent in their household. Her father was never there. When he was, he shared too much and did not ask enough about Joy. She found herself being the one helping her brother with homework, cleaning the house, and cooking if they wanted something other than takeout. She often felt like a substitute wife but did not know how to change her circumstances or feel confident enough about her assessment of the situation to voice her unhappiness.

When Joy came to therapy, she was very hesitant about examining the complicated dynamics of her relationship with her father. Furthermore, she had buried her conflicting emotions about her parents' marriage and the impact of their actions on her childhood and her ability to feel safe in her home and depend on the adults in her life. Her anxiety was a reflection of her keeping a lid on so many conflicting and complicated emotions and thoughts, which she did not have the ability to even begin addressing. Furthermore, she thought her ADHD was rooted in her using all of her emotional resources to keep a lid on the neglect and psychological abuse she had experienced. She did not have anything left to give to high school or her friends. These internal struggles were externally perceived as her difficulty in concentrating, zoning out, being impulsive and irritable, having trouble completing assignments, and memory issues and forgetfulness. As you may recall from the previous section, these symptoms are also a sign of trauma.

When Joy shared what was going on, it was clear she felt ashamed and helpless about her struggle to manage everything and at the prospect of disappointing the adults in her life. In line with Joy's tendency to take on overwhelming responsibility, she approached her mental health like a problem to solve, leading her to research her issues and self-diagnose. Unfortunately, as can commonly happen, she was not accounting for the chronic and persistent trauma she had been experiencing in the form of neglect and toxic stress.

On top of this, Joy had deeper trauma that she had not put into words even for herself, never mind someone else. Over the course of therapy, she gradually realized that her parents' issues were not her fault or responsibility. She started connecting with her anger and frustration around being misled and taken advantage of by the adults who were supposed to be protecting her. It took a while to break through the denial and defences she had built to bear her mother's estrangement. She was loyal to her father to a fault and struggled to tolerate any negative feelings towards him. As she progressed towards accepting these difficult emotions, it paved the way for her to be able to recall and tolerate thinking about the deeper, buried trauma she had experienced. This involved a couple of incidents of her father assaulting her. While she remembered what happened, she could not reconcile these incidents with her father. They had never spoken about what had happened, and he never acted inappropriately towards her outside of those situations.

In therapy, when she finally had a trusted adult to confide in, she began to put these pieces together out loud. Like many victims of abuse, Joy struggled with the idea of 'speaking badly' about an abuser who was also someone she loved. At times her defence mechanisms flared up, making her want to take the blame for the abuse instead of feeling conflicted about her father. Being able to acknowledge that her father had abused her led to a period of grief over her parents and family. Yet, it also allowed her to bring aspects of buried trauma to light, which were deeply interfering with her functioning, even though she could not name or identify the root cause of the symptoms she had been experiencing.

In actuality, disclosure has been found to play a vital role in recovery from trauma. It is best if it occurs in the days or weeks following a trauma, but disclosure at any point, even years later, has a positive impact on the outcome of someone's recovery.[102] According to Sloan and Wisco,[103] disclosure is most effective if it happens over multiple occasions and is detailed and specific. The purpose of disclosure, as in Joy's case, is to organize someone's experience in a helpful way, dispelling erroneous beliefs (i.e., 'It happened because I drank too much.') In this manner, the person reconsiders the events that happened with a professional or trusted person. The end result is a more empowering and cohesive narrative, which, with the right support and therapy, can result in a story of resilience.

In the alternate situation, people choose not to disclose their trauma. The problem here is that if they have chosen not to disclose because of shame or guilt, they can develop a negative core image of themselves and erroneous beliefs about the trauma and themselves. Research has consistently shown that trauma can negatively impact one's sense of self.[104]

When we choose to keep things to ourselves out of shame and guilt, we do not feel better. Instead, these things tend to grow in the darkness of our minds, feeding erroneous beliefs and fears. These thoughts commonly show up as statements like, 'I should have done more', 'I caused this somehow', 'I will never be worth anything anymore', 'No one will love me if they know this.'

Take, for example, Morgan, who came to see me after months of suffering in silence. He came to therapy only because he could no longer handle the weight of his thoughts and what they were doing to him. He was avoiding his friends, could not look at his parents, and had trouble finding any motivation to engage in college and the sports he lived for. Once an easy-going young adult, Morgan felt that his life was over, and he would no longer have the dreams he had worked so hard for. Morgan shared that his values meant a lot to him. He had worked hard in high school, trained hard for sports, and held himself up to a high standard in his friendships. Morgan was quite naive when it came to relationships and girls. He had been prioritizing other things and was waiting for college to start dating. He had not so much as kissed a girl, despite getting a fair bit of attention from them. That is why Morgan felt so ashamed when he stayed the night at a female friend's house after a party and was assaulted. Morgan had been asleep when the inebriated female friend climbed into bed with him. She tried to get him to engage with her multiple times in increasingly direct ways. Morgan tried to brush her off but felt frozen, as her attempts became pushier and more forceful. He told himself that she was drunk and condemned himself for making such a big deal of things. Inside, he felt trapped, knowing that he had no way home that night, as it was the middle of the night. He tried to make it obvious that he was asleep and hoped for her to get the point and fall asleep as well. She did not. In the end, Morgan ended up staying frozen as she took advantage of him. Afterwards, he turned around and went to sleep, as did she. He was deeply ashamed and humiliated. He was terrified of what she would tell their shared friends. He downplayed every feeling that what had happened was an assault. He felt emasculated and embarrassed. He vowed to never tell anyone and tried to put it out of his mind.

For some time, that worked, but not for long. As we have seen in previous examples, what is buried has a way of showing itself eventually, even if a person does not make the connection to events, thoughts, or emotions they have buried as deep as possible. Morgan tried to throw himself into the same activities that he had enjoyed before. He tried to stay busy with friends but found himself looking for signs they knew what had happened. He was afraid they would judge him for having hooked up with this particular girl. Worse still, he was afraid that she would twist the story of the night and make him feel even more emasculated than he already did. When he was at home, he had a hard time feeling the usual motivation and engagement he had towards his life. His parents had started noticing something different about him, which only served to make him withdraw more to avoid questions. He felt increasingly alienated, which only fed the increasingly negative thoughts about himself. By the time he came to therapy, he had internalized many of the negative thoughts and fears he had. He strongly believed that he would not be able to live a normal life again, that his friends and parents would distance themselves from him if they found out, and that he would never find the same joy and hope he previously had regarding his future. The negative thoughts Morgan had about himself are, unfortunately, typical and reflective of the common thoughts trauma survivors have. The experience of the trauma and the ensuing thoughts become so overwhelming when left buried that individuals lose their sense of self and self-worth.

This is particularly the case for long-term and chronic trauma, such as prolonged childhood abuse. Chronic and lasting trauma, which begins at a young age, takes place at the same time an individual's identity is forming. We previously spoke about how insecure attachment goes on to impact a person's view of themselves, others, and the world. Earlier, we have discussed how childhood and intergenerational trauma impact the genetics and brain development of children. If you consider these different pieces, it does not seem surprising that trauma and its subsequent mental and physical impacts alter the development of one's identity, especially when occurring at critical developmental periods.

Individuals with a safe and supportive childhoods who have secure attachments to at least one healthy adult grow up to seek connectedness, fulfilment, and love in their lives. Without trauma, they are freer to trust the world around them, which allows them to take chances and go after the things they want to achieve. Seeing themselves succeed in the goals they pursue is a reinforcing cycle that allows them to believe in themselves further and reach for higher pursuits.

On the other hand, individuals who have been through lasting trauma that shapes the development of their identity around itself have been shown to value seeking safety, surviving, and minimizing abuse. Where some may see opportunities for excitement and growth, a person with chronic trauma sees only obstacles and fear. Where a person who has grown up in a safe and nurturing home sees new people as new friends or playmates, a child of abuse sees people who can hurt them or get them in trouble with an abusive parent. Growing up as a child who has experienced a form of lasting abuse can shape the way they view and interact with the world in several different ways, but all are organized around resolving the abuse and correcting the narrative of being traumatized.

However, without support, a person may be doomed to repeat the same actions, such as being attracted to destructive relationships or keeping themselves isolated from others for fears of safety. In these cycles, people's actions further their sense that the world, themselves, and others are not to be trusted. This reinforces the cycle of feeling disconnected from others and being defined by their trauma and negative thoughts about themselves.

Our role in therapy is, firstly, to reestablish safety and a safe environment for individuals. Secondly, it is to reassure clients that the shame, guilt, and feelings of low self-worth they are experiencing are products of the traumatic event and not caused by them doing anything wrong or by them being less worthy of love and a fulfilling life. Targeting these insidious and deeply rooted negative thoughts for the tricks they are involves a considerable amount of therapy. This is usually done as part of cognitive behavioural therapy (CBT). We will talk about CBT and the impact of negative thoughts in chapters seven and eight.

Chapter 5

Family Dynamics

> 'It is now clear to me that the family is a microcosm of the world. To understand the world, we can study the family: issues such as power, intimacy, autonomy, trust, and communication skills are vital parts underlying how we live in the world. To change the world is to change the family.'
>
> —Virginia Satir

Few people shape us more in life than family, whether it is in negative or positive ways. This chapter will start by focusing on the impact of siblings and birth order as well as the narratives fed to us when we are raised being compared to other family members. We will look at the larger family legacies inherent in nuclear and extended families and the impact of a family's mental health on us as individuals. The perceived roles of family members in one's life and how we grow into new roles (like, mother) will also be focused on in this chapter. These roles are often key to people's mental health and cause them to seek therapy when they realize the similarities between themselves and those who played these roles in their lives.

Family Legacies

The families we are born into have legacies, similar to epigenetic changes and the intergenerational trauma of our ancestors. Family legacies are stories, beliefs, attitudes, and values passed down from one generation to another. They are things we grow up with but might not be aware of until we are older and reflect on them. They are another form of buried information, often accessed unconsciously. They impact us, regardless of whether we are aware of them. Often, we do not confront our family legacies until we create our own families and consider the values, beliefs, and attitudes we want to teach and pass on to our own children. Being aware of family legacies allows us to consciously reject and accept the parts of them we want to uphold and pass on to future generations.

Family legacies can be either positive or negative. Thus, they can enable us to strive towards fulfilment and meaning or hold us back from pursuing certain experiences, achievements, and ways of being. These legacies become an inherent part of our identities. Sometimes, they allow us to develop full and complex identities. Other times, they hinder the development of our identities, making us feel incomplete or stuck. Our identities are narratively formed, meaning they are made up of the stories we construct, embrace, and reject together with others to make up our lives. The family is the first point of origin for creating and sharing stories with children, which they incorporate into their perception of themselves, the world, and others. Family stories told repeatedly and passed down the generations go on to form legacies. These legacies have been found to be most influential for teenagers and young adults who are going through a dramatic shift in developing their emerging identities.[105]

Emerging adults are individuals between eighteen to twenty-five years of age who are coming into adulthood. During this time, individuals take their family stories and legacies and incorporate them into how they see and interact with the world. This is an important point to consider, as young adults today are quite different from how they were several generations ago in terms of expectations, goals, and values. Instead of adulthood being reached by getting married, it is now focused more on individuals' characters, responsibility, and their ability to make independent and appropriate decisions.[106] The legacies they choose to accept, reject, or embrace are core components of their identities and how they interact with the world and others.

In another way, legacies work to preserve family identities—at least the stories we embrace and accept as part of our families' narratives—over time and generations. Stories about how our families have survived and found fortune and happiness through work inspire us while others warn us of the dangers that may lay ahead and invoke fear of certain experiences. Stories that make up legacies are powerful in that they give us a sense of cohesion and joint meaning. Family legacies can be incredibly empowering and connecting, pushing us to face fears and issues while making us feel secure in the strength and support of our family. Let us take a look at examples of family legacies and the ways in which they can be expressed.

Positive Family Legacies

1. Honouring quality time together: This type of legacy includes holiday traditions, fun, yearly vacations, valuing frequent communication, etc. It can influence an adult to nurture, commit to, and prioritize relationships in their lives, aiming to have a family of their own in which they create a culture of spending positive and enjoyable time together.
2. Family first: This involves working to maintain positive and supportive relationships.
3. Reaching for the stars: This leads people to push towards goals and achievements, valuing success, education, hard work.

4. Taking care of others: This involves helping each other, community service and volunteering, valuing communities, being a good citizen, and charity.
5. Overcoming all obstacles: This helps people survive distress or trauma, valuing personal and emotional strength.
6. Being grateful and thankful: This encompasses an optimistic attitude towards life, discouraging complaining or asking for more, and difficulty accepting needs when they clash with circumstance.
7. Always keeping promises: This means loyalty, dedication, putting a lot of weight in your word, and working hard.

There are many possible ways in which positive family legacies can be expressed, some stronger and more influential than others. If you look at the above examples, you may realize that even positive legacies can be conflicting and have negative consequences in some situations.

For example, take the case of Charlie and Meredith. They came to couples therapy after seven years of marriage and having two young children together. Charlie had a strong family legacy about the women in his family. He had been raised by a single working mother who had been raised by a single working mother as well. Growing up, Charlie knew they struggled financially and could see how hard his mother worked to make ends meet while supporting Charlie and his sister. Despite working hard, she always kept the house clean and provided her children with home-made meals.

When Charlie met Meredith, he was captivated by her free spirit. She was unlike anyone he had met before. They never ran out things to talk about or adventures to go on. They had a blissful relationship till their first child was born, and they found themselves frequently arguing over minor things. In our first session, Charlie expressed that he still loved his wife very much but was feeling increasingly resentful that he took on more household responsibilities and felt that he took on a greater load of the active parenting, such as taking his children to activities and out to play.

Charlie was the working parent in the relationship, and his wife was unable to work due to her being a dependent on his visa, which only granted him permission to work. Despite knowing this fact, logically, he could not help feeling that she did not live up to his expectations of a mother. He found this to be even more so the case when his mother came to visit, and he witnessed her ability to take over caring for the household.

Charlie and Meredith's situation is a prime example of why awareness of family legacies is important. If we took this situation at a surface level, we may come to a different conclusion about Charlie and Meredith. Realizing that Charlie's resentment is deeply rooted in a family legacy gives the situation a different context that we can work with. Charlie had chosen Meredith for himself based on the individual values he started to develop as an adult—prioritizing quality time, being active, adventurous, and open minded. These were values he could not have fulfilled in his earlier life, as their family had been centred around being stable and meeting basic needs. What Charlie did not realize was that he had formed a core image of what a mother did and provided for her children based on his early childhood experiences.

This made him overlook the ways Meredith looked after and provided for their children in a different capacity. Meredith was fun-loving and connected with the children. She made time to nurture their interests and find them activities and events to take part in. She made sure they had dinner as a family together and always spent quality time together on the weekends. She was neither as tough externally as Charlie's mother seemed nor did she prioritize soldiering through her day at all costs. Instead, she taught and practised taking care of herself and modelled gentleness and nurturance to their children. There was much validity and strength to Charlie's family legacy, and there were certainly aspects of his mother's and grandmother's values and beliefs that he wanted to share with his own family. However, his attachment to his family legacy was too rigid and did not allow him to see that his new family had different needs, styles, and ways of being. Keeping this legacy buried and out of his full awareness meant that his resentment towards his wife grew, instead of his flexibility towards his own family.

Additionally, understanding Charlie's family legacy allowed Meredith to understand and have more compassion towards the things Charlie asked for. Instead of feeling judged for not doing enough and obligated to be a certain type of mother, she was able to account for some of the behaviours that appealed to Charlie, such as cooking on special occasions and being more active while playing with the children.

This example shows that it is important to be aware of our family legacies and to realize that we have the agency to revisit and revise them. We can change aspects of legacies that do not work for us and reject aspects we have lived by without rejecting the whole story. However, this cannot happen without complete understanding.

Negative Family Legacies

On the other side of positive family legacies are negative family legacies. There is equal value in examining and being conscious of them. Negative family legacies can include erroneous beliefs that hold us back, limit us, or can be as detrimental as ideas rooted in racism, sexism, or discrimination. The problem with these types of family legacies is that since they are shared by a group of people, discriminatory ideas or harmful beliefs can be normalized and accepted, giving individuals more power to stand behind and pass on hateful ideas. Here are some examples of such legacies:

1. Parents are always right: This includes punishment, disregarding the emotions and safety of children, not allowing individual choice, and strict and rigid discipline.

2. Family first: This often means devaluing others, not allowing outsiders (i.e., partners) into the family, teaching children to put themselves before others at all costs, unhealthy competition, and need to win.
3. Outsiders cannot be trusted: This includes not trusting or communicating with others outside of a community, race, or religion, low tolerance of otherness, disrespecting others' beliefs, mocking, discriminating, or hurting people who do not share the same values or characteristics (i.e., skin colour, religion) that the family has prejudice against.
4. Take what we need: This encompasses a disregard for rules or laws, encouraging breaking rules or violence, cheating, lying, and devaluing others.

Negative family legacies are often inculcated by children who observe and learn the behaviours of adults engaging in unhelpful or destructive ways. The power they hold is connecting people through the blame, criticism, or admonishment of others. While these legacies may bring a family together, they do not do so in healthy, nurturing, or empowering ways. They limit potential and growth and can feel particularly hard for a person to go against.

Remember, a family legacy is not a determined sentence or path for an individual's life. An individual has the choice and power to be able to examine their legacies, just as they can evaluate whether the people around them support their mental and physical health, fulfilment, and growth.

Signs that You are Being Negatively Impacted by Family Legacies

1. You are rigid and inflexible towards growth in certain areas.
2. You and your partner experience recurrent conflict over parenting or joint decision making.

3. The way you guide your children ends up causing more distress rather than helping them.
4. Your family cuts ties with outsiders easily.
5. It is hard to allow new members into the family.
6. You find it difficult to connect with others.
7. You react disproportionally to small issues.

Uncovering Your Family Legacies

- Take some time to consider the stories you have heard from your parents and grandparents.
    a. What is the moral or value of these stories?
    b. What is the speaker emphasizing?
    c. What is the speaker proud of?
    d. What lessons are they trying to teach you about your family?
- What sayings or principles—like never leave the job undone, we do not quit, always be early—do your family repeat?
- What are your family's attitudes towards itself?
- What are their attitudes and beliefs about others outside of the family?
- What kind of actions do they approve of? Which do they disprove of?
- How do religious and political views impact the identity of your family?

Take some time to consider these questions. If you can, speak to parents, siblings, aunts, uncles, and grandparents. You will see the legacies start to form. Then, consider how these legacies have impacted you.

- Which of these help you grow and meet your potential?
- Which of them help you feel fulfilled?

- Which of them connect you to others and your community?
- Which of them have held you back from connecting to others or trying new things?

Now, think about the values and beliefs you would like to have.

- What would you like to pass on to your children or teach them to value?
- What stories would you like to live by?

Identify a list of limiting and erroneous beliefs and values. Work on paying close attention to challenging these beliefs. Consider what your life would be like if it was not guided by such inherited beliefs? Push yourself to act differently from erroneous beliefs. If you need help, a therapist can work with you on this.

The important lesson here and in previous chapters is that we are born and, along the way, bury and disconnect from certain aspects of ourselves, our families, and our identities. Much of this is just out of our awareness and is waiting to be discovered. But we have the power and ability to bring this information to light and change our paths forward, finding the glory of the knowledge and legacies we embrace. Bringing information to light means you can actively reject and accept the principles and values you choose; you can use awareness to work on the aspects of yourself that need help and support. Most importantly, you can make a different life from the aspects of your history that hold you back.

Siblings and Birth Order

In the early nineteenth century, Alfred Adler, an Austrian psychologist, first studied birth order. Adler posited that the order in which children are born in a family (birth order) and the size of a family result in certain predictable positive and negative incomes for children. In essence, each child experiences their own environment and experience within the same family based on their birth order. The four categories of birth order that are thought to result in significant differences in outcomes are firstborn, middle child, youngest child, and only child.

Adler's work prompted a continuous stream of research based primarily on the relationship between birth order and personality, intelligence, and achievement. In terms of personality, the characteristics that have been frequently researched and thought to vary according to birth order are extraversion, emotional stability, agreeableness, conscientiousness, and imagination. Some studies have corroborated the differences while others have found that birth order has a limited impact on us.[107]

Outside of personality, intelligence, and achievement, birth order has been shown to impact risk taking behaviours and substance use. Specifically, a study of 946 Chilean children found that firstborns score greater on IQ tests and have higher intelligence while being better protected against developing substance abuse problems.[108]

The Chilean study begins by pointing out the impact of culture on birth order. Specifically, certain cultures, like those in Southeast Asia and South America, emphasize on firstborns in terms of obligations, expectations, and familial role. This is especially the case for firstborns who are expected to care for the family, financially and physically. In this way, firstborns take even more of a parentified role and are encouraged to continue in their parents' footsteps. Sometimes, this means getting into a certain, family-approved profession. Other times, it means running a family business. These expectations are beneficial in providing a supportive framework for individuals to follow but can be overly rigid, impacting mental health and causing conflict within the family.

Studies on birth order in Asia and Southeast Asia specifically are still extremely limited. Research on Asian Americans has shown that interdependence is central to the family, with closeness in sibling relationships and harmony being prioritized well into adulthood.[109] Research shows that connectedness and closeness is a protective factor against sibling rivalry and negative treatment from parents. This means that siblings in Asian cultures are closer and feel more favourably about each other, eliminating some of the competition and negative feelings that can be encountered in other cultures. Studies on firstborns from Asian American families corroborated that they felt expected to assume family responsibilities and pressured to be a role model to younger siblings but had the additional view that having siblings who shared similar, less traditional views like them was a great comfort and allowed for more independence.[110]

Take, for example, Annabelle, who is a Chinese Malaysian firstborn female who came to therapy with her fiancé, John, after he found out she had been giving her family money again. This had been a point of contention between the couple for some time and was exacerbated by John struggling because of how much time Annabelle spent with her family. John felt that they were not being allowed to be their own family or decide how they spent their time. When he found out that Annabelle had been giving money to her parents and younger siblings, he worried about what this meant for the family they wanted to start together. This culminated with John finding out that Annabelle was in the process of taking out a mortgage on behalf of her parents, which she would pay for the next thirty years.

John was rightfully upset about finding out these details but felt conflicted about how upset he could feel. John also belonged to a Chinese Malaysian family. However, he had spent most of his growing up years in the UK. He came to understand that Annabelle felt considerable pressure as the firstborn of her family, especially because her younger siblings were not in stable jobs yet. Annabelle had long taken an over-parentified role with her siblings. Due to the large age gap between herself and her siblings, she had grown up being accustomed to the idea that she was one day going to take financial and emotional responsibility for her aging parents and younger siblings. Therapy focused on helping John understand Annabelle's beliefs and values, and he came to understand that taking on these responsibilities was an important part of who Annabelle was. It was not wrong of Annabelle to adhere to the path her parents had raised her to follow or to prioritize the closeness that was a part of her family legacy. However, Annabelle had to work through therapy to understand that she also had an obligation to communicate honestly and share important decisions with her fiancé. She learned to have more compassion and understanding for John instead of feeling controlled by his asks to spend more time together. John saw Annabelle work hard to make room to prioritize their family by giving them space for quality time together and discussing decisions before she made them. This allowed him to account for her wishes towards her family, and they were able to financially plan their future in a way that incorporated looking after Annabelle's family and their own.

Conversely, European American families have trends of siblings who may be less involved with each other as they enter adulthood because they value independence. This is a common trend there in comparison to Asian cultures and focuses on families raising their children as individuals with their own passions, ambitions, and goals. The benefit of promoting independence as a parenting style is that there is the potential for less conflict when children focus on their individual goals and paths. Yet, the decreased emphasis on joint decision making and prioritizing family unlocks the potential for weaker attachments. It is important to consider that there are many factors that can come into play to moderate the relationship between sibling order and closeness, thus resulting in different outcomes. Let us now look at the characteristics of different birth order positions.

Firstborns

For a period, firstborns benefit from the undivided attention and nurturing of their parents. On one hand, they experience trial and error parenting while their parents navigate parenting for the first time, but on the other hand, they experience the undivided investment of their parents to a level that cannot be competed with for subsequent children. Due to the high level of expectations from them and investment in their upbringing, firstborns tend to be ambitious, conscientious, and hard working. They tend to be high achievers and, in fact, have been shown to have a small but significant IQ advantage.

Some studies have found that each increasing birth order position results in a statistically significant decrease in IQ.[111] These characteristics, along with increased familial support, mean that firstborns end up being leaders and trailblazers, often tending to complete higher degrees and aiming for more rigorous professions (like medicine and law). The theories behind this pattern point to them having more resources to share as well as them growing up in a more stimulating environment, in which they have more interactions with adults in general.

Due to being first, they enjoy a period of being an only child, which lasts until the second child comes along and they are 'dethroned'.[112] Through the process of another child being added to the family, a firstborn acquires more expectations of being responsible and sharing in care taking of subsequent children. Additionally, they can become more conscientious and take on a parental role with middle and younger children. Firstborns may behave this way, partially, to gain parental favour, which can be perceived as a limited resource. A firstborn's advantage is their part as a role model, caregiver, and source of knowledge and information for their younger siblings. Coupled with the parental push to achieve and succeed more, firstborns often actively help in the upbringing of younger siblings. This may be a role they embrace or resent, sometimes oscillating between the two.

Characteristics of Firstborns

Firstborns are:

- most likely to follow parents' thinking and beliefs,
- high achievers,
- ambitious and conscientious,
- likely to complete higher degrees and aim for more rigorous professions,
- trailblazers,
- trusted with more responsibility,
- fearful of failure,
- less likely to take part in dangerous sports,
- more rigid,
- more likely to seek attention.

Middle Children

Middle children are often portrayed as the rebellious ones. This rebellion does not have to be a bad thing because, often, rebellion means acting and thinking differently from the parents and the firstborn. The middle children carve out their own space by doing things differently from those that came before them. If we look at the fact that firstborns are given more attention and resources, it follows that children born later have to carve out their own niche, which is different from others before them, to command attention. As a result, they tend to be creative and adventurous. They are more self-reliant and tend to take things as they come. Part of being the middle child is understanding your place in social dynamics more and, thus, being more adept socially. The even tempered and socially knowledgeable middle child often attempts to keep the peace.

Sometimes, this can have the downside of them being people pleasers or too tuned into empathizing with the needs of others. Middle children rely more on the social support of others, as they receive less non-essential parenting from caregivers who are splitting resources between more than one child. This does not mean a middle child is any less loved or cared for, but it comes down to resources. However, this can be perceived as an unfair advantage of division of resources and attention by a middle child.

Characteristics of Middle Children

Middle children are:

- rebellious,
- aware of not getting as much attention as their siblings,
- can feel undervalued,
- likely to have less cognitive support,
- may have less non-essential parenting.

Youngest Children

Youngest children tend to think outside the box in an attempt to carve their own niche. They take a more carefree approach to life and feel a lighter weight of responsibilities. Studies looking at the mental health of younger children generally point to better mental health, with some conflicting information based on geographic location. Studies in Asia, such as one assessing adolescents in Japan in 2021, have shown that youngest children tend to show higher levels of resilience, self-esteem, and happiness. Some studies in western countries like the US have shown higher rates of happiness among youngest children.[113] Other research coming out of western countries, like the UK and Scandinavia, have also found an increase in psychiatric problems like depression, anxiety, and suicide attempts.[114] The rise in psychiatric problems among younger children has been consistently attributed less to financial and socio-economic resources and more to struggles for parental attention, along with a potential for less supervision. Research on birth order in Chinese Americans and Korean Americans shows the inverse pattern among firstborns. They have shown higher levels of depression and anxiety due to greater pressure to fulfil their familial obligations and responsibilities.

Characteristics of Youngest Children

Youngest children are:

- likely to seek more attention,
- playful or fun-loving,
- outgoing,
- likely to be self-centred,
- social,
- good at making social connections on their own,
- adventurous,
- likely to struggle with not being the first to achieve something,
- less disciplined due to easy-going parenting.

Only Children

Only children benefit from being the sole focus of their parents' attention and affection. They do not have to compete for attention, favour, or resources with siblings. Thus, they do not see peers as competition the way children with siblings do. They can be thought of as 'super firstborns' who are often ambitious, diligent, conscientious, and focused on being high achievers. Thus, they encompass the traits of firstborns listed above. Because of these traits, they often take the role of leader in social and professional settings.

Characteristics of Only Children

Only children are:

- perfectionists,
- conscientious,
- diligent,
- leaders.

Family Size

In addition to birth order, family size is an important factor influencing personality. Families with smaller sizes have more attention and resources to split among family members. A family of three will have a different make-up in terms of resources, attention span, and structure than that of a family of seven. It is important to contextualize the attributes associated with birth order with the impact of family size exaggerating them.

Knowing individuals' birth orders in their families is another way of identifying how they fit into this world and what shapes their lives. Individuals' perception of their birth order is equally, if not more, important than the impact of their birth order. Some middle children may take on the role of the firstborn depending on the characteristics of the firstborn and whether they have any physical or mental health issues that intervene with their ability to take on the assigned role. For example, if a firstborn is chronically ill, has a developmental disorder, or a mental health issue that interferes with their ability to succeed, their younger sibling may assume the role of the firstborn. Overall, knowing the characteristics of birth order can help individuals evaluate how they interact with the world and their families—their place is not set in stone.

Questions to Ask Yourself

- Based on the values identified in the previous section, do you see a relationship between your birth order and accepting or rejecting family values?
- What is your perception of parental favour in your family?
- Do you identify with your birth order position? What parts of it do you identify with?
- What aspects of your birth order position would you like to change?

Familial Mental Health and Substance Abuse

The mental and physical health of our families profoundly impact our development and level of fulfilment and success across life. Although the level of risk varies depending on the position in the family (child, sibling, or spouse), research consistently shows that family members are impacted by the health of their family members and have significantly higher rates of physical and mental illness themselves.[115]

When an individual is experiencing mental health issues in a family, the family acts as the first point of caregiving and support. Often, mental health and substance abuse issues take time to manifest. Family members are often the first to recognize and face the consequences of such issues. This initial reckoning with the issue occurs without outside support and with limited information or support around it. During this time, the family of the afflicted member may feel isolated and helpless, and they may worry and feel anxiety about the family member's suffering and their responsibility to help the affected member. This impact is exacerbated by the severity of the substance abuse issue or mental illness, and if the afflicted person belongs to low- or middle-income countries, with limited mental health support, where the burden of caregiving falls more heavily on family.[116]

Researchers have examined the perception of the family burden of mental health and substance abuse issues as a key factor in influencing an individual's personal well-being and mental health.[117] In this research, family burden is defined as, 'All the difficulties and challenges experienced by families as a consequence of someone's illness.' This includes the emotional experience of an individual who has a family member suffering from mental health issues, as well as the financial, physical, and emotional cost of caregiving.

Caregiving, in particular, has been consistently related to higher rates of depression, anxiety, insomnia, and burnout.[118] There is a greater risk of negative mental health outcomes among those caring for spouses over those caring for parents or siblings. Women have been found to experience more mental health difficulties while men report more caregiver strain.[119] In general, younger individuals and the unmarried report suffering more from familial burden when taking over caregiving responsibilities.[120]

Children of people with mental illness have been found to be at a greater risk of developing mental and physical health issues, although this risk can partially arise from genetic vulnerability, stigma around mental illness, and financial difficulties when caring for parents with mental health issues. In terms of significant mental illness, like schizophrenia or bipolar I disorder, it has been found that socio-economic drift and financial and emotional disadvantages are related to experiencing divorce, separation, loss of employment, and disability in the future. These issues last into adulthood and can impact people's mental health and quality of life later on.

For example, Peter came to therapy with relationship problems. He had issues with commitment and difficulty thinking about the next steps of his relationship. At the time, Peter was fifty-four and had not been in a serious relationship, until he met Angela. On the surface, Peter seemed and felt like he was ready for a committed relationship, which included living together and marriage. However, when it came down to taking action, he felt terrified. When searching for the root of Peter's problem, it became clear that it was linked to his mother's mental illness.

Peter's mother had schizophrenia. Growing up, Peter had not been aware of the extent of his mother's issues. Like most women who develop schizophrenia, she did not experience her first psychotic break until she was nearly thirty years old, at which point Peter was approximately ten years old. As he reached his teens, he became aware of his mother's paranoid thinking. She would think their friends and family were collaborating to take their money and imprison her. She grew increasingly reclusive and introverted. Peter had an image of his mother as gentle and loving. He could not help blaming himself, as many children of parents with mental illness do, for what his mom was experiencing. He tried to help her feel safe and spent as much time as he could with her so she would not feel alone.

During this time, Peter's dad—Peter's only stable support—threw himself into his work. He said it was to help the family and cover the costs of his mother's hospitalizations, which were becoming more frequent. But Peter could not help feeling that he was trying to get away from them, especially as Peter's mother started to voice that his father could not be trusted either or was conspiring with his parents to take her away. Peter's perception of reality blurred during these days with his mother. It was hard for him to know when she was his reliable mother and when the things she was saying were a product of mental illness. It was even harder for him to feel grounded and gain perspective because he had become isolated during the time he spent with his mother, as she had cut off family members due to paranoid thoughts. The strained relationship between his mother and father meant that Peter was even more alone and struggled to develop an accurate and healthy perspective of his family's mental health issues. Unsurprisingly, Peter started feeling anxious and depressive, most of which went unnoticed until a counsellor stepped in during his junior year of high school. At school, Peter was quiet and did not have any close friends, but he was friendly enough with teachers and classmates. He did well at school and never acted out in any way. Thus, they did not notice that he maintained a distance because his mother's fears of others had started to get to him as well.

The counsellor stepped in when Peter's mother was hospitalized after a particularly bad incident, and his teacher noticed him falling asleep in class. The counsellor was able to intervene with Peter's father to encourage him to attend college in another country, so he could be surrounded by a frame of mind different from his mother's. Peter thrived in his school in the UK. He gradually made friends and enjoyed having his own space. From this point onwards, Peter's life could have been very different had it not been for an incident between his mother and father. Without Peter around as her main support, Peter's mother's mental health had deteriorated, leading her to become increasingly aggressive towards Peter's father and resulting in the police being involved one day when she went at Peter's father with a knife. Peter's father told Peter about this incident and urged him to come home, as he was going to leave. Peter left university and returned home to Malaysia. His worry about his mother and his parents' separation triggered a breakdown, which changed the course of Peter's mental health. From that point on, he had trouble carving out his own life and committing to anything that could lead him away from home and being his mother's caregiver. He developed deep rooted trust issues about others and knew that his mother would deteriorate without him.

When he met Angela, he wanted to build his life with her as he had been capable of doing in his university days, which remained the best time of his life in his eyes. Like many children of parents with serious mental health issues, Peter increasingly struggled with the idea of independence from his sick parent.

His financial prospects were limited by him leaving university early, and the financial resources he had from his job were used to help his mother. He could not imagine how he would emotionally separate from being his mother's caregiver, never mind financially be able to do so.

Angela only knew the tip of these issues. Although Peter cared for Angela, he also did not know how to be genuinely honest and transparent with her about his life and mother. He had never seen a secure attachment or a mature and mutually loving relationship. He only knew how to be a caregiver in a relationship and did not have the capacity to be another person's partner until he began to delve into these issues.

Therapy focused on helping Peter understand his distorted and deeply mistrustful thinking patterns towards others. He began to address his trust issues with Angela. This led to more insecurity, as we realized that part of Peter's attraction to Angela had been based in taking care of her as she struggled with her own health issues. Angela and Peter's relationship had to be redefined from one of caregiver and receiver to one of equality, where they could mutually look after each other. This led to a necessary reconsideration of their goals together and an agreement to considerably slow down their commitment to taking steps towards moving in together and getting married. Instead, they committed to help each other grow and develop their mental health first. This prioritization and change in commitment allowed Peter to be more open with Angela and let his anxiety about commitment diminish. When I last saw them, they were making peace with being in a committed relationship without having to push for the next steps, adhering to a timeline they perceived as obligatory.

In Peter's case, his mother's mental health issues triggered his vulnerability to paranoid thinking and anxiety. However, the consequences of caring for her through her mental illness significantly influenced his life's trajectory and related sense of well-being. Due to the impact of his mother's mental illness, Peter experienced the strain and separation of his parents' marriage, estrangement from his extended family, isolation from peers and other safe adults, and the impact of increasing financial scarcity. When he was growing into adulthood, Peter was influenced by his mother's distrust of others and their community, which stayed with him in the form of trust issues later in life.

Children who have a family member or parent with mental illness, like Peter, need early intervention and support. Up to 50 per cent of such individuals report some kind of physical, economic, or mental health consequence.[121] This is especially the case for vulnerable populations like children, single parents, and lower income households. If family members can be properly educated about the battle they will face and the toll it will take on themselves and their families, proactive decisions can be made to provide children and family members with opportunities to grow and thrive while treating mental illness. Early intervention—programmes to support childhood activities, socialization, and counselling for both children and their parents in terms of parental guidance, psychoeducation, and social support—is critical to lowering the risk of negative consequences. Knowledge indicates to guidance counsellors and workplaces to provide further relief, as individuals caring for the mental health of another family member may be too overwhelmed to know when they are in over their heads.

Another similar situation exists in families that have one child who is mentally or physically unwell in some way, resulting in increased focus, resources, and attention being given to the 'sick child'. When one child starts showing symptoms of a long term or chronic mental or physical health illness, an initial period of confusion, fear, and uncertainty ensues for the whole family. Parents may try to shield other children in the family of the details to protect them. The tension and anxiety of the household can often be felt by all individuals, despite parents' attempts to shield children. In fact, it can be better to give age-appropriate explanations to children instead of shielding them. Shielding can lead to internalization of behaviours and feelings of self-doubt, blame, and fears about the family and sick sibling, and somatic complaints like stomach aches and headaches.

Overall, siblings of those with chronic illnesses report higher rates of anxiety and depression, experiencing fears related to their sibling's future. This cumulatively takes a toll on siblings, manifesting through social problems at school, in friendships and extracurricular activities, and while trying to have fulfilled social lives.[122] In addition to internalizing such issues, such siblings can exhibit external signs of being affected, such as verbally or physically aggressive behaviour, acting out, or behavioural issues like refusing to go to or skipping school, tardiness, not completing assignments, or being disruptive in the classroom.

These symptoms can increase the level of overall family stress and lead to frustration towards the struggling sibling. Alternatively, factors such as chronic illness can shift how birth order is expressed in a family and can result in a youngest or middle child assuming the role of a firstborn. For example, if a firstborn or older sibling develops a chronic illness, the middle or youngest child may feel an increased responsibility to take on parenting or caretaking roles. This can lead to a sense of hyper responsibility and pressurize the middle or youngest child. Such children may struggle to draw boundaries, over assume responsibility, or be drawn to other people with whom they can take up a caretaking role.

Let us take the example of Robin. He came to therapy as an adult because he was feeling unsatisfied and unfulfilled in his life. Robin was the second of two children, making him the youngest. When Robin was twelve, his older brother met with an accident that led him to be hospitalized for the better part of a year. Prior to this time, Robin's brother or parents would always be at home with him. But, suddenly, he found himself home alone while his parents would alternate between working and spending time at the hospital. Robin would frequently come home to an empty house and had to learn how to take care of his daily needs like dinner and completing his homework. Robin was kept in the dark about much of his brother's struggles in those early days. He would worry about whether his brother would make it. When Robin's parents returned from the hospital, they would look worn down and defeated but always put on a brave face for him. Robin knew that his parents felt guilty about leaving him on his own, but without any relatives living close by, they had little choice. Robin hated making them worry and felt he could not tell them how much he feared being on his own. He was also scared that a car accident similar to his brother's would hurt his parents one night when they were tiredly driving home from the hospital. He tried to look after himself as much as he could and hid his growing anxiety from his family.

His brother faced a long journey and rehabilitation process once he got home. When he returned home, Robin tried to take as much as the burden of looking after him off his brother. He showcased his growing skills in the kitchen and stayed ahead of his homework and academics in a way that he had never cared to before. He spent time with his brother, especially when he felt guilty that his brother could not celebrate the same occasions and events that Robin had ahead of him like school plays, friends' parties, and sports games. Robin became very good at downplaying his needs and anticipating the needs of his family. He was not unhappy, but as a young adolescent, he thought he was stronger and more mature than he was in actuality. His armour was a false sense of self-sufficiency and suppressing his needs and difficult emotions.

As he grew into an adult, Robin began to feel unsatisfied with his life and relationships. He came to therapy unable to pinpoint the source of his dissatisfaction but shared that he did not enjoy certain patterns in his relationships and work life, which left him feeling taken advantage of and uncomfortable. When Robin described his life, it became clear that he was drawn to situations and relationships in which he believed someone was being treated unjustly or needed extra help in their lives.

He shared that at work and in his personal life, he frequently found himself fighting battles for others. This could range from sticking up for someone who had been treated rudely in a meeting or taking on tasks that were another department's responsibility to getting involved with women who were emotionally unavailable or not over their past relationships yet.

However, Robin struggled to advocate for himself. He was able to see where he should set limits and boundaries in his relationships and at work, but it took very little for him to capitulate and bear the brunt of the responsibility. At the time, Robin would feel happy that he was able to make a difference, but this feeling would not last long. Ultimately, he felt unappreciated and found himself wishing for reciprocation. During therapy, he mentioned being unhappy with work, burdened with too many projects and handling tasks that should be handled by other departments. While he had taken on tasks outside of his role to be helpful, his intention had been to get a head start on important tasks before they were taken over by the appropriate person or department. Instead, he found himself spread thin and increasingly frustrated with his words falling on deaf ears.

Robin's personal life mirrored his professional one. He was involved with a woman who leaned on him for emotional support. She was everything Robin hoped for in a relationship. But she was still working through the damage caused by her previous relationship. Over time, Robin realized that her ex-partner was still the primary man in her life and that, although she was interested in starting a relationship with Robin, she would not be able to reciprocate his feelings.

Helping Robin meant coming to understand the role he played in his family. Robin was used to being the person who took the initiative, looked after others, and fixed problems. He was keenly in tune with the emotions, moods and needs of others from years of de-escalating his brother's anxiety or dysregulation and attempting to soothe his parents in times of worry. He had a hard time making himself a priority when he had been trained to prioritize the struggles of others. When he did ask for what he needed, he felt guilty and anxious about the impact his perceived neediness would have on the relationship. Understanding these dynamics was key in helping Robin understand his role and responsibility in perpetuating his problems.

Robin was attracted to situations in which he played the same role he did in his family. Being there for someone, making a difference, activated his attachment system in a way that felt familiar and, thus, rewarding. Through understanding the deeper, buried roots of his problem, Robin was able to start addressing the fears, worry, loneliness, and anger he had felt, as a twelve-year-old and adolescent, towards his brother's situation and his family. He had never allowed himself to entertain these internalized worries and had buried his fears deep down. Addressing them in therapy allowed him to bring them into conscious awareness and let go of them. It also allowed us to see the full extent of the anxiety disorder he had developed. Subsequently, we worked on easing the impact of anxiety by challenging and correcting distorted thinking patterns and erroneous beliefs.

Siblings of individuals with mental health problems are more vulnerable to experiencing emotional issues and cognitive problems, like hyperactivity and difficulty focusing. Similar to Robin's case, adolescents aged fourteen to seventeen have been identified as the most influenced by emotional issues, with about 50 per cent of mental health issues being established by the age of fourteen[123] with symptoms ranging from those mentioned above to more significant ones, like psychosis. This could be due to the increased awareness of consequences and appreciation of the future that adolescents of this age start to develop. This awareness can result in increased worry about their siblings' future and recognition of the impact a higher needs sibling has on their family environment and future. This is further complicated by the fact that kids this age tend to internalize problems and turn to the outside support of peers rather than confiding in their parents. The other age group found to be most influenced by a sibling or family member's mental health issues is that of younger children, who are most impacted by changes in caregiving, unrest at home, and instability in the family.

As can be seen, the mental and physical health of the family is something that we have to factor into care and supporting children and families. Research shows that this is especially the case for siblings of children with rare illnesses—like Prader-Willi syndrome, Fragile X syndrome, Noonan syndrome, and Duchenne muscular dystrophy—90 per cent of such children have anxiety and psychiatric disorders like generalized anxiety disorder, obsessive compulsive disorder, separation anxiety, panic disorder, and social anxiety disorder.[124] This staggering number points to the importance of early intervention at the point of diagnosis to help family members circumvent the impact of living with patients of chronic illnesses on the mental health of vulnerable youth.

In Robin's case, his parents responded to his brother's acute trauma and chronic issues much like the way other parents of children with a life-changing illness do. Such parents report feeling anger, helplessness, hopelessness, diminished energy and face cognitive issues like forgetfulness, distraction, poor concentration, and lack of focus on other aspects of their lives. These cognitive issues are, in large part, related to focusing on the sick child, worrying about the sick child's future, and thinking about other children in the family. This is a time where the impact of one's community and extended family can make a significant difference to how hopeful or helpless people feel. Those with limited community support often feel left behind and increasingly alienated from the lives of friends and family who do not share similar lives focused on the chronic illness of a child.

How Roles Change Over Lifetimes

We have looked at some of the important ways in which the social dynamics of our families make us who we are, the kinds of problems we have, and how we experience relationships and interact with the world when we are adults. Another way in which we are shaped in our lives is the changes in our roles from birth to adulthood. So far, we have focused on childhood and the roles we are assigned at that age, which determine what future roles we assume as partners, spouses, or parents.

There is evidence of our personality traits changing over our lifespan based on the roles we take on.[125] Certain traits seem to change with age, maturity, and responsibility. An example of this is introversion, as studies have shown we become more introverted after marriage. Furthermore, research shows that personality changes based on the degree to which we invest in certain institutions, such as family, work, and religion.[126] Most personality traits and changes are based on the framework of the 'big five', which are five personality domains we are all thought to have. These are extraversion, agreeableness, openness to experience, neuroticism, and conscientiousness.

The five main personality traits have been outlined below:

- *Extraversion:* Liveliness, sociability, ability to be outgoing vs reserved or solitary
- *Agreeableness:* Cooperativeness, kindness, helpfulness, compassion, ability to be friendly vs critical or judgmental
- *Openness to experience:* Imaginativeness or curiosity vs cautiousness or reservation
- *Neuroticism:* Moodiness, sensitivity, or worry vs resilience or confidence
- *Conscientiousness:* Discipline, hard work, reliability vs carelessness or inconsistency

Traits like neuroticism, openness to experience, and extraversion decline across an individual's lifespan while those like agreeableness increase. Conscientiousness increases until middle age, peaking around the age of forty to fifty, and then starts to decline later in life. In terms of neuroticism and agreeableness, emotional maturity and perspective gained with age allow one to increase characteristics of agreeableness while becoming more emotionally stable and, thus, decrease neuroticism.

Personality changes have been theorized to develop similarly across the world. These changes across individuals, lives have been found to occur in different cultures from the US to China to Belgium to Russia.[127] Personality changes that come with age are attributed largely to changes in physical health and cognitive ability, which alter openness to experiences and sociability.

Quality of life and health vary greatly across cultures, which is thought to explain cross cultural changes in personality traits due to aging. Studies have compared American and Japanese populations in terms of personality development and found two important differences. First, in a country like Japan, health is significantly better in older age than that of other well-developed countries, as Japan holds the record for longevity in terms of age worldwide. Second, Japan has much more variation in personality development based on social factors. For example, the pattern of conscientiousness varies in Japan where social duty may become higher priority than career in midlife, leading to lower levels of conscientiousness.[128]

Personality also changes in response to important life events occurring and changing the way we think about life, priorities, values, and goals. We have spoken about how this can happen in response to mental and physical health issues and to changing positions within our families of origin. Other times, this may occur after marriage or becoming a parent. Getting married and embracing parenthood come with major shifts in role that impact our identities in ways that are difficult to predict ahead of time.

However, by thinking of our families and that which has shaped us along the way, we can do the work to become aware of the psychological challenges we may develop and learn how to deal with them ahead of time.

Entering a marriage or a committed relationship begins the process of becoming 'we' from being 'I'. This is often a thrilling and exciting new time, which can also feel like a threat to one's independence or awaken buried fears related to marriage and commitment. Transitioning from an individual to a family unit is considered an identity shift. It can cause individuals to experience positive and negative symptoms and bring about changes that they may not think about much due to the business of the time. Significant positive personal growth and increase in fulfilment can occur around this time. For many, starting their own family reflects them achieving their life's goals and leads to the fulfilment and connectedness they have been looking for.

Studies have found higher rates of depersonalization around personal identity during the process of marriage,[129] which we may bury. Identity shifts such as marriage and becoming a parent are both transitions that allow for identity exploration and changing social circles and dynamics. Growing up, many are aware that they want to do certain things differently from the way they were raised or have a specific vision for their family with goals and attributes they aspire to. For example, someone who lived in an abusive or neglectful household may strongly prioritize the emotional safety of their children. They may pay special attention to educating their children about abuse, danger, and proper boundaries. In the family, the focus would be on creating an environment where a child can feel comfortable discussing mistakes, asking difficult questions, and expressing negative or vulnerable emotions. While choosing a partner, the emphasis could be on picking a person who responds to their needs and validates them through emotional support. The process of establishing one's own family can be a corrective life experience, which allows them to move forward from the experience of coming from an abusive family. However, to be able to have this corrective experience, awareness of their past circumstances and their impact on a person is necessary. For this to be successful, a person must do the work to acknowledge and process their own trauma before being able to use their awareness to create a different, healthier future for their family.

When someone gets married or becomes a parent, they have to re-evaluate their histories and the roles their parents played as a married couple and their parents. Parents' decisions, frustrations, and rules take on new meaning. What they could only understand through compassion and perspectivizing before becomes their lived experience.

For example, let's look at Fatima. Fatima was a forty-year-old Malay woman who came to therapy because she had started having panic attacks. Fatima had neither experienced a panic attack before nor had she considered herself particularly anxious. While describing her life, she explained that she had a happy adulthood, with a long-established career in international relations and felt fulfilled in her life with her husband and twelve-year-old daughter. She was perplexed about having panic attacks, with the first occurring weeks before bringing her daughter to boarding school.

Fatima did not know she was experiencing panic attacks, like many others who experience a sudden onset of a panic disorder, because she was exhibiting physical symptoms without awareness of the psychological and mental processes. Often, clients come to therapy for help with panic attacks after believing they suffered from a heart attack or stroke. After ruling out physical causes, physicians send them to psychologists, having recognized the tell-tale signs of panic attacks. For Fatima, this included: racing heart, dizziness, clammy hands, chest tightness, and feeling like she was going to pass out. In fact, she had been experiencing some of the physical symptoms of anxiety, such as numbness, tingling, and shortness of breath since a year while her anxiety at the prospect of having a serious medical condition heightened. Like many others who have panic attacks or a panic disorder, when Fatima's anxiety reached an all-time high, her body signalled to her mind that she could no longer live as she was, burying unprocessed aspects of her past and relationships.

In fact, many people who start having panic attacks later in life consider themselves to be easy-going and not too anxious. It is not until they examine their lives, sources of stress, and influential experiences that they understand they have been dealing with anxiety through denial and compartmentalization. Fatima succeeded as an adult but struggled in her family life prior to the age of thirteen when she went to boarding school. Her parents were often dismissive and invalidating and did not foster close and supportive relationships. Fatima learned from a young age that she was an inconvenience to her parents and that she would benefit from making herself as invisible as possible. Her parents were encouraging about her accomplishments related to school and sports, which offered rare glimmers of the kind of family life she had hoped for. However, Fatima did not bring her problems to her parents. She also did not confide her dreams or goals in them. When she was sent to boarding school, she understood she was being banished from the home and began to look forward to starting her own life.

At the age of eighteen, she did exactly that, taking the first job that would get her out of Malaysia and allow her to live on her own terms without being dependent on her parents. At the age of forty, she moved back to Malaysia for the first time as an adult to help her ailing mother. Once again, Fatima was sharing her space with her mother and had taken on a caretaking relationship with her. Her husband had to stay back in the UK for work and only came to visit while her daughter chose to go to boarding school in the UK. It became apparent that buried, unresolved emotions and issues from her past were coming up now that she was sharing her space with her mother and experiencing a parallel situation with her daughter going to boarding school as she had. She had left her family at a young age and started something better for herself but had never faced what she left behind. With her mother's frail condition, she began to feel a level of empathy and regret about their relationship. However, like most things buried, Fatima did not realize the full impact living in this situation would have on her.

During therapy, we quickly realized that Fatima had been experiencing anxiety and depression for the year that she had been living with her mother. Fatima had not recognized that her difficulty leaving her room, wanting to constantly sleep, and irritation when speaking to her family were symptoms of depression. Instead, she felt a growing sense of guilt about not being present with her daughter and acting impatiently. We were able to examine Fatima's role as a mother living with the conditions of her childhood. We discussed Fatima's instinctive fleeing from her home to protect her sense of self-worth and create a life and family she felt loved and fulfilled by. Fatima was able to recognize that becoming a wife and mother had been a turning point in her life, which allowed her to reinvent herself and cultivate the relationships she wanted. She worked hard to be a present and active mother. She recognized that she easily felt guilty when it came to her child but dismissed these feelings as normal. It was not until she was faced with both her mother and her daughter in the same setting that she became hyperaware of the want to be by herself, the irritation and impatience she experienced when her daughter asked her for something, and the immense, unprovoked anger she would feel at times.

These feelings were not Fatima's but rather her parents' displaced emotions. Like many buried emotions, they were disconnected from her. It was only in therapy that she began to understand how her role as a mother had been forming for the past thirteen years and was partially informed by her own unresolved experiences. Fleeing her past would not provide the permanent escape and resolution to her past, which she had blindly hoped for. Facing the change in her role from an unseen daughter to a struggling mother made her see her mother from a different perspective.

She came to understand that her mother had been abused by her husband and, as a result, had no voice in the decisions made about Fatima. Giving Fatima affection and attention had resulted in the noose of Fatima's father's control tightening around her mother. Fatima, of course, had not understood that her mother's disengagement from her was related to her mother's struggle to survive. She began to feel more compassionate towards her mother, which made her rethink her childhood and the role her mother played in her life. This brought to the surface many unpleasant and overwhelming feelings, which led to panic attacks. However, tackling her conflict began the process of redefining herself through motherhood. Fatima was able to understand what she carried into motherhood and use her new awareness to reclaim her identity as a mother. Some of her new identity was certainly based on her history and her own mother, but it was still rooted in her choices.

Through healing open wounds with her mother, Fatima was able to address the trigger of her panic attacks. She had perceived her daughter's decision to attend boarding school as a rejection of herself as a mother, which caused her to question her parenting. Fatima's greatest fear was that she would not have a strong connection with her daughter and that her daughter would want to escape her the way she had fled from her parents. As Fatima's family never discussed problems or spoke about emotions, Fatima learned to identify and express her emotions. Ultimately, this process helped Fatima and her daughter have open conversations and ways of relating, which they had not broached in the past. Fatima came to understand that her daughter had picked up on her withdrawal from the family and realized that Fatima and her mother had issues she was not privy to. Ultimately, this process brought Fatima and her daughter much closer together.

As can be seen from our discussion so far, the past is not a life sentence. Like Fatima, individuals can come to terms with their childhood experiences to create a better, more fulfilling life.

Chapter 6

Grief and Loss

> 'Your body is not a coffin to bury your grief in.'
>
> —A client who lost someone to suicide

The loss of a loved one has consistently been found to be the most stressful life event that we face as humans. The first empirical study on grief happened in 1944, after the Cocoanut Grove Nightclub fire took 492 lives in a mere fifteen minutes. It has been classified as the deadliest nightclub fire in history. Erich Lindemann, a psychiatrist who specializes in bereavement, began studying the tragic event after seeing the grief and traumatic effects on the Boston community in which the accident occurred.[130] At the time, Lindemann was working at Massachusetts General Hospital, which treated the majority of injuries from the fire. What he witnessed and his subsequent research paved the way for our understanding of grief. Lindemann and his staff had initially been perplexed when patients in the emergency room started being angry and aggressive, some going so far as kicking those trying to help. Until then, we had no recognition of grief and its behavioural and psychological symptoms. We certainly did not know what to expect ahead of time when mass casualty was involved.

Lindemann hypothesized that individuals struggle with living with the loss of something important, whether this is another person or a part of themselves. He noticed a predictable cluster of physical symptoms, including exhaustion, heaviness of limbs, chest and throat tightness, and waves of physical pain. Psychologically, these patients expressed intrusive thoughts about their loved one, anger, guilt, and hostility towards others and themselves. He labelled this cluster of symptoms 'acute grief'. He quickly found that acute grief was experienced not only by individuals but also by communities and those who have to support others to heal.

Fast forward to the present day, we have come to understand grief as distress and anguish experienced after the loss of a loved one. Grief can be felt upon the death of a loved one, the end of a relationship, a traumatic separation, or the loss of or transition away from a part of oneself, which can include identity, change in socio-economic status, imprisonment, or loss of functioning due to health or injury and more.

According to Lindemann, reactions to grief also include separation anxiety, yearning, confusion, sadness, anger, psychological distress, apprehension about the future, and feelings of hopelessness.[131] These symptoms are all considered to be part of the 'normal' grieving process, which diagnostically can last up to six months. Even though symptoms tend to start feeling more manageable, a person's loss is felt over the course of their lifetime, as they encounter reminders of and learn to live without the person they lost. It is important to note that nothing about 'normal grief' feels normal. It feels devastating and painful. Yet, thanks to research, we have managed to find patterns in how grief is typically experienced. Statistics show that 50 to 85 per cent of individuals experience 'normal' grief after a loss, but as many as 15 per cent of individuals only express minimal symptoms in the year or two after a loss.[132]

When people come to therapy to address grief, it is usually soon after they have experienced the loss. I have seen many different expressions of grief, all of them have been 'normal' because everybody grieves differently. Some are keen to talk about the person they have lost, remembering the good memories and the things they loved about the person as easily as the details of how they lost them. Others shut away the good memories as they try to cope with their pain and avoid talking to others about what they are experiencing. Some are angry while others cannot accept the loss. In my experience, everyone struggles with whether they are grieving 'appropriately'. When people get remarks like they 'look better' or 'seem like their old selves', people in therapy often express the worry that they are doing their loved one a disservice by not mourning enough. Others worry that they will never be able to feel complete again.

Most people receive well intentioned comments from friends and family that can make them feel supported and hopeful or just as easily serve to leave them feeling severely disconnected from others. Some people experience the greatest difficulty in their separation from the loved one and the pain it brings. This awareness and pain comes in bursts of twenty to thirty minutes for most people, which feels overwhelming and acutely disorienting. Over time, the stage of acute grief, which comes with overwhelming distress, turns to internalized grief. More positive feelings start being intermingled with the feelings of loss and pain. These may be related to moments of relief, reflecting on positive memories and stories about life before the loss or related to living the present life. Experiencing positive emotions and memories has been shown to reflect resilience and better recovery in individuals six months after the loss.[133]

There are many factors that come into play in the grieving process. A person's relationship with the individual lost, lacking the opportunity to properly mourn, or witnessing a traumatic death greatly impact what grief looks like. Complicated grief or bereavement is a form of grief that has similar symptoms to normal grief but impairs an individual's functioning and is much more distressing. Complicated grief occurs in around 10 per cent of grieving individuals who do not move from acute to internalized grief.[134] Often, a person experiencing complicated grief may feel it to a distressing degree for a much longer time, obliterating their ability to function.

For example, grief can become complicated if the person's relationship with the deceased is difficult. Someone who is estranged from a loved one or experiencing conflict can also grieve. Such grief is difficult to predict the course of and is experienced in unexpected ways by the individual.

For example, let us look at the case of Ani and her mother Shannon. Ani was a difficult child who, in her teens and adulthood, developed narcissistic personality disorder (NPD). It is marked by a lack of empathy, need for admiration, and feelings of grandiosity. People with NPD seek admiration and attention, often at the expense of others. On the outside, they portray an exaggerated sense of self-importance but on the inside, they suffer from feelings of low self-esteem and self-worth. People with this disorder greatly impact family and friends, making stable relationships difficult to achieve. They put immense strain on their families, as they actively need to be the centre of attention (whether good or bad) and view the world in distorted ways, supporting their belief that they deserve special treatment. Often, this entails them relentlessly asking for money, which they feel owed, from family members, using abusive language, becoming enraged and physically violent when needed, and being manipulative in relationships. Understandably, this takes a toll on relationships over time as family members and loved ones feel powerless to set boundaries with the person.

Shannon was on the receiving end of her daughter Ani's abuse since her daughter turned eighteen. She was a single mother who worked hard to make ends meet and felt immensely guilty for not spending enough time at home. She tolerated Ani's harsh comments and criticisms for years, feeling that it was her fault her daughter felt like she was not there for her. When Ani started tearing up her relationships and threatening Shannon that she would call the police or hurt Shannon because she did not give her money or her time, Shannon realized that her daughter had a real problem. Shannon spent time in therapy, seeking advice on setting boundaries with her daughter, none of which worked. After Ani tried to sue Shannon and took all of her money, self-worth, and sense of hope, she made the conscious decision to cut ties with her daughter. This is a common outcome of relationships with individuals who have NPD when they refuse to seek help and the condition keeps escalating.

This estrangement took a devastating toll on Shannon. She stood by her decision to end her relationship with her daughter but suffered the impact of her grief for a long time. Her grief made her doubt who she was as a parent and as a person. She went through bad and good days when she struggled with her decision of not calling her daughter. Her grief was compounded by knowing her daughter was out there, not dead, and that she had self-imposed this sentence.

Shannon's grieving process took several years to resolve. She lost her resolve at times and saw her daughter, who continued to contact her for money. She, at times, felt bad when her daughter reached out from a new number or through a relative saying she missed her and that all of the things Shannon had wished had come true. She particularly struggled on Mother's Day, birthdays, and holidays. Over time, she learned the hard way that even her daughter's nice words were a manipulative tactic to get back into her life because of what Ani could gain from her.

Ani never felt any remorse for her actions. This was a relationship that would never change. Acceptance is often said to be a major healing step in grief—acceptance of what has been lost and how the future will be different than imagined. This acceptance was hard to reach for Shannon, but with some help and support, she was able to get there.

However, Shannon's grief would return whenever she heard through others that her daughter was struggling, which leads us to the day Ani was killed in a fatal accident. Shannon did not expect to grieve to the level she did when she found out about Ani's death. When she did, she was certainly not prepared for others who knew her situation voicing their surprise and disbelief about her grief. Shannon struggled with how she portrayed her grief (mourning) and internalized much of it. She often felt that she did not have the right to grieve anymore while other days she realized that despite being estranged she would always be Ani's mother.

Shannon's grief turned into what we now classify as persistent bereavement disorder. Persistent bereavement disorder is diagnosed when a loss has occurred over twelve months ago, and the symptoms of grief experienced by the bereaved are still intense enough to interfere with their functioning. It is more likely to happen in cases with complicated grief, after a series of losses, with lowered social support, while experiencing other significant life stressors, among individuals under the age of sixty and those with a history of depression and/or negative and distorted thinking patterns. Shannon had struggled with depression and negative thinking since the estrangement with her daughter. So, now, she was struggling with her perceived responsibility in causing Ani's death. Returning to therapy, Shannon had to deal with a fresh grief while also addressing the loss of identity she felt and the wish that her daughter would have received the help she had needed.

We can also look at Shannon's grief as 'disenfranchised grief', which occurs when an aspect of grieving or the loss goes against what is socially accepted. Shannon did not feel she had the right to grieve her daughter to the extent that she felt the loss because of her decision to cut Ani off in the first place. This view was reinforced by others who felt that she should have moved on from her relationship and did not understand or support her grief. Shannon neither received phone calls and messages of support nor did people check in on her and provide her food or help. She was going against societal expectations and this lack of support, like with others with disenfranchised grief, led to deeper feelings of isolation and loneliness.

Other examples of disenfranchised grief could be an LGTBQ+ person losing a partner who was not approved of by friends and family, getting an abortion, experiencing the end of a difficult or toxic relationship, or having someone they love imprisoned. People may not understand the depth of their grief or falsely believe that their grief is not appropriate in these situations. Disenfranchised grief can lead to greater internalization of symptoms that, on the surface, may manifest as the person being occupied with work, unwilling to meet for social activities, and outwardly lacking emotions about the loss. Internalizing and burying grief symptoms lead to a higher risk of substance abuse to cope and are likely to result in self-harm or thoughts of suicide unlike those who receive support and help while grieving.

Traumatic grief occurs when bereavement is disrupted and complicated by a traumatic death or loss, such as in a suicide or sudden accident. Traumatic bereavement or grief is not a diagnosis in itself but incorporates elements of normal grief with symptoms of PTSD. Essentially, in these situations, the person experiences symptoms of depression and trauma, such as intrusive reexperiencing, avoidance and numbness, hypervigilance, mood instability, hyperarousal, and emotion dysregulation. When experiencing traumatic grief, people are likely to have more severe symptoms of depression, including suicidal thoughts, which could qualify as a diagnosis of a major depressive episode or disorder.

Let's take a look at the story of Pearl. She sought therapy after losing her closest friend to suicide. Pearl had a history of depression (major depressive disorder), which she had been struggling with since becoming an adult. Her friend, George, had struggled with his own depression. At times, they could only rely on each other to understand when suicidal thoughts felt overwhelming and other times only they could know how to bring each other out of a difficult place with a specific mix of humour, solidarity, and non-judgement. Suffice to say, Pearl felt a level of responsibility for George, in the same way she knew he felt responsible for her. George, no doubt, knew this as well and took steps to hide his plan to attempt suicide from her. He took care to make sure she knew there was nothing she could have done. This is the case for many individuals who have decided to take their lives and made a plan—they reach a level of resolve and peace that can be confusing to others. Friends and family report seeing their loved one in better spirits and often having no indication of what was coming. When Pearl found out what had happened to George, she spent a significant amount of time feeling guilty about not having helped him, torturing herself by poring over their conversations, wondering if she could have been there more or said different words that would have made the difference.

Each time Pearl felt like she was coming closer to understanding how things happened and finding some relief, she would find herself experiencing acute grief after discovering a new detail. First came a letter addressed to her, explaining how to handle some of his affairs, next came some of his important belongings in the mail, then a visit from his girlfriend who had uncovered new details. Pearl dealt with a back-and-forth process of understanding that George had made his choice and feeling retraumatized all over again by details of the suicide and George's level of pain. She struggled with accepting that he was at peace versus trying to provide details to his family members, who were morally against suicide due to their religious beliefs.

Pearl experienced a significant depressive episode during this time. She struggled to motivate herself to engage with her life and think about her future. She struggled with intrusive thoughts and images of what had happened. Additionally, she worried about her own future and felt scared about where the suicidal thoughts she had experienced in the past would lead her.

Over time, Pearl showed incredible strength in her ability to keep her friend's memory alive in a way where his personality, kindness, and fortitude shone through. She arranged a memorial for him. Bringing together different people from different areas of George's life, she created the celebration of his life as she knew he would have wanted, and she sang a song that he had always loved. These actions helped her make peace with his loss and understand that he would have wanted her to move on. One day, in therapy, she put it especially well when she shared the sentiment, 'Your body is not a coffin to bury your grief in.' Pearl approached most things with a level of creativity and eloquence that helped her process and accept an unfathomable loss. George's death ultimately came to motivate her to takes risks to make her life fulfilling and meaningful in ways she had difficulty taking the leap with. While she missed George greatly and mourned him deeply at times, he was very alive in how she chose to live her life moving forward.

Coping with Grief

Learning to cope with grief means learning to connect with what was lost in a meaningful and substantial way. The initial loss and separation are a devastating blow, yet it is not and should not be the end of the relationship with the lost person. After accepting the loss of a loved one, a person must transform the relationship into one that has several levels such as 'actual, symbolic, internalized and imagined relatedness'.[135] Essentially, this means reimagining the relationship while accepting the physical part of the relationship is over. As we have seen in the past chapters, much of the physical and psychological consequences of mental health issues come with what is buried and not brought to light. Denying a relationship with the lost loved one or lost piece of identity, past, etc., constitutes a denial and compartmentalization of an important part of someone's life. It is tempting for many to put the lost person in a box to live their lives and not be overwhelmed by the pain. However, it is a temporary solution that causes more pain and loss in the long term. As with many buried issues and emotions, they come to the surface in one way or another, through physiological and psychological symptoms.

Overall, finding ways to create and have a new relationship with the lost person greatly predicts the manner in which someone moves out of the acute stage into internalized grief. Grief has the capacity to render someone functionless. Research shows that grief causes cardiovascular changes, such as increased heart rate, variability, systolic and diastolic blood pressure, higher levels of cortisol, and dysregulated HPA axis activity.[136] Important changes in the immune system, lowered immune response to vaccinations, and increases in inflammation are also characteristic of the grief processes.[137] Perhaps the best-known illustration of physiological risk to health is the 'broken heart syndrome', which is the phenomenon of married or partnered widows succumbing to heart issues in the six months following their spouse or partner's death. In medical literature, this phenomenon is called Takotsubo cardiomyopathy, which is cardiomyopathy induced by acute stress, which results in the ballooning of the left ventricular apical. This is commonly known as death by a broken heart.

Clearly, this is a more extreme example of the physiological consequences of grief but shows the range of severity while facing trauma and grief. Support, therapy, and the interjection of hope through building awareness and forming a meaningful relationship with what or who was lost make the difference in outcome.

So, how do we redefine our bond with a lost loved one? This act can be highly subjective as there is no wrong answer. Many people see signs of their loved ones around them, such as thinking about what they would do or say in a given situation, memories as reminders, or even finding familiar ways of thought or action as their loved one in others. Here are some ways to foster and continue your bond with a deceased loved one:

1. Maintain relationships with the individuals who were important in your loved one's life. Speaking to people who knew your loved one as well as you provides support and allows you to get to know them in ways that you may not have before. While your family and friends play an important role in providing comfort and support in the aftermath of a loss, they may not know the loved one or grieve their loss to the extent you do, which, at times, can feel isolating. Share photos, reminders, thoughts of your loved ones with their families and friends. If what you lost is not a person, identify people who remind and connect you to the part of your life, place, or aspect of your identity that you are grieving.
2. Write letters to your lost loved one. This can serve two purposes. The first is to provide a way to maintain contact, sharing all of the things and experiences which you would if you continued to share a physical life together. The second is to address unfinished emotional business. This can be particularly helpful if a loss was sudden, and you did not get to share important sentiments or thoughts. In some cases, particularly with complicated grief stemming from conflicting relationships, letters can serve the purpose of apologizing, voicing forgiveness, or sharing things you never had the chance to.
3. Think about what your loved one valued and the legacies you want to hold on to and live by. What mattered to them? What lessons did they share with you? What stories and sayings did they repeat? We often know what our loved one would say or do in a situation and that advice and knowledge can bring great comfort at moments of distress. Sharing these stories, sayings, and values with friends and family helps them keep them alive and supportive of the impact they have on your life.

    If you have children with the lost person, sharing their legacies allows them to get to know their lost parent in developmentally appropriate stages as they age. This is also true for children who may have lost a beloved sibling. Children who lose a sibling or parent may struggle with their limited memory or knowledge of that person, especially as they grow up and their awareness increases. In situations like this, they can be affected by the lack of an enduring bond and the unknown in ways in which buried information has an internalized impact on us. Natural ways to continue legacies include establishing traditions, sharing their stories, and keeping photos and mementos of the person. This is also applicable to when the loss does not involve a living thing; carrying forward traditions and legacies from life before continues a relationship.

4. In line with continuing legacies and establishing a bond, continue an activity or passion of a loved one. Examples of this may include running a yearly 5k in their honour or supporting a cause related to their death, going on the trip of a lifetime they always spoke about, completing an experience important to them like climbing a mountain or hike, learning the piano, or starting a garden.

5. Think about the ways you felt closest to the loved one or thing. Simply think of these moments and incorporate them into your life in ways that comfort you.

6. Set up a foundation, scholarship, or event to honour the life of a loved one. If your loved one enjoyed reading, you could set up a yearly donation to a library. If they were a college professor, you could start a scholarship in their name. Other examples include volunteering your time, fostering or supporting children or animals. Remember, there is no minimum limit or specification that makes a cause or contribution worthy.

7. Honouring a loved one does not always have to be financial. Planting a tree with your children, visiting and

taking care of the lost one's grave, making their famous recipes on a special occasion all constitute ways to honour a loved one and mark an important milestone. Make sure to give yourself the opportunity for privacy and personal space, while also identifying people to reach out to for comfort on milestone days. It is common for the ways in which people feel to take them by surprise on such days, particularly during the first year on the anniversary of the death, birthday, or a milestone like the due date of a stillborn child or a miscarriage. There is no right way to feel at such times. To some, it does not feel emotional, as they expect it to, which may trigger ensuing guilt and others may feel physically ill or unable to focus on work or their usual activities. Make space for yourself and honour the day in the way you see fit—nothing is too small.

Part III

What We Do Not Know, We Do Not Know

So far, we have discussed the circumstances and experiences we inherit, develop, and encounter that create the blueprint of our lives and shape who we are along the way. Our focus has been the impact of the knowledge, emotions, legacies, and narratives we keep out of our awareness and the impact of doing so on our physical and mental health. Now, we turn to look at the mechanisms, maladaptive coping strategies, and distorted thinking and beliefs, which keep this knowledge out of our consciousness at a price.

Chapter 7

Defence Mechanisms and Maladaptive Coping

> 'She has a steel exterior, but it protects a candyfloss heart.'
>
> —Kristin Hannah

This chapter gets into the specifics of the mechanisms we unconsciously use to repress our lives and knowledge in a misguided attempt to protect ourselves. These defence mechanisms and maladaptive coping styles are often creative, intelligent ways for children and individuals who would not be able to cope with their experiences to survive.

Defence Mechanisms

We use defence mechanisms as a way to cope with everyday problems, external threats, and inner conflict.[138] They are unconscious reactions meant to protect us from anxiety by keeping distressing information buried and outside our awareness. They can be seen as unconscious coping strategies, which differ in the sense that defence mechanisms are unconscious while coping skills involve conscious knowledge and behaviours.

These defence mechanisms are hierarchical and range from immature to mature, with mature defences being more adaptive and helpful with coping in a healthy way. The more immature a defence mechanism, the more it distorts reality and hides important information from us. For example, denial is frequently considered the most immature of the defence mechanisms, which completely distorts or blocks the disturbing reality of a situation. Whereas, in opposition to this one, the more mature defence mechanisms, like humour and suppression, redirect and moderate the stress associated with the information without blocking important knowledge.

The blocked information can include thoughts, memories, facts, and emotions. However, even the most immature defence mechanisms have a protective purpose. Denial can be useful in the same way as dissociation when circumstances or emotions are too overwhelming to bear or there is no foreseeable way out of them. Situations like chronic abuse, significant medical issues, or substance abuse can all provoke the use of denial. For example, a person abusing substances usually suffers from an increasing need and tolerance for higher amounts of the substance. At the same time, the behavioural changes associated with using the drug take a toll on the person, their relationships, and other aspects of their life, like work. They are mostly unaware of this, with individuals telling themselves that they can control or stop their drug use when needed. You can tell an individual is in denial when they refuse to acknowledge their role in an issue, avoid it, blame it on someone or something else, and minimize the extent of the problem. Denial is dealt with by bringing awareness and taking responsibility for the issues. However, straightforward confrontation with a person usually backfires, as much of denial is unconscious and has a protective barrier, which, when breached, can trigger anger. Instead, a mix of empathy and challenging the accuracy of beliefs and behaviours can begin a process that brings the unconscious material to awareness to start the process of recovery. Making a person feel safe, supported, and hopeful makes an overwhelming truth easier to face and helps them see a way to overcome.

It is important to note that all of us use defence mechanisms at times and that their protective value is something we often need to be able to deal with issues in a manageable, piecemeal manner. Sometimes, we do not have the luxury of allowing disturbing or difficult knowledge to stop us in our tracks or deter us from caring for families, interfering with work, or simply surviving the conditions we are experiencing. When we frequently use immature defence mechanisms or fall into a pattern of using defence mechanisms without realizing the need to confront what we are burying and examine our psychological functioning, we run into problems.

Similarly, it is common for children and adolescents to use defence mechanisms, especially when they are learning to manage and identify emotions, developing a sense of moral integrity, and forming their identities. These tasks involve bringing knowledge into awareness and learning how to actively cope with the resulting emotions. For example, adolescence is a time when individuals face many new challenges and a higher intensity of social and academic demands. Variation has been found in coping strategies in relation to factors like gender—women have been found to use defence mechanisms that involve internalizing and active or purposeful coping skills seeking social support. Using defence mechanisms like regression, altruism, somatization, and reaction formation, women have been found to turn more hostile or negative sensations into positive feelings to help others to offset their discomfort. Maladaptive or unhealthy coping skills and defence mechanisms used by women tend to include being hostile to themselves, which can lead to increased anxiety and depressive symptoms.[139]

In opposition, adolescents boys use externalizing defence mechanisms such as acting out or experiencing and expressing anger related to distressing knowledge. Anger, in many situations, can feel validating and protect from more vulnerable negative emotions such as sadness and hopelessness. In this way, anger gives individuals a way to cope with the situation without feeling the full paralysing impact of the associated distress. When overwhelming negative feelings come to the surface, men and boys use defences like suppression, which come across as looking unemotional or being mistaken as uncaring. In general, adolescents use more strategies to minimize the impact of the new demands, challenges, and emotions they experience through defence mechanisms, like suppression, repression, and inhibition, while developing into using more prosocial strategies like altruism and reaction formation.

Commonly Used Defence Mechanisms

Rationalization: This can be quite a protective defence mechanism in that a person does not fully distort reality. When using rationalization, a person comes up with justifications and logical explanations for unacceptable feelings, wants, or needs. For example, if a person does not get the job they have been working for, they focus on why it was not a good fit for them.

Intellectualization: In reaction to overwhelming information, like the loss of a loved one, a person avoids difficult emotions by focusing on the logistics and rational aspects of the loss. For example, the person may focus on the medical details of the loss, arranging the funeral, and organizing the estate of the lost loved one in a rational and proactive manner. A person using intellectualization can appear emotionally detached or uncaring, yet this strategy allows for a person to pace out the processing of the loss and deal with difficult emotions in a more manageable manner. The difficulty is when the emotional aspect of the issue is not addressed, as emotions provide important information about a person's functioning and motivate them to address issues.

Reaction formation: This defence mechanism is used by a person who expresses the opposite of their needs, emotions, or wants. Usually, this happens because they feel uncomfortable about that need, want, or belief. For example, a person abusing substances frequently talks about drugs being bad or a teen who has a crush on a classmate acts like they do not like them. Protests and opinions are often exaggerated. This is outside of the person's full awareness and can lead to problems accepting themselves and who they are.

Compartmentalization: This is one of the most frequently used defence mechanisms. It involves separating difficult emotions, thoughts, or beliefs that contradict each other. It is a lesser form of dissociation. It can be helpful in the short term, as it allows someone to separate a conflict from consciousness to focus on other things. However, compartmentalization is often responsible for the buried information causing physical and emotional symptoms that bring someone to therapy. Having this information segregated from consciousness takes a toll on the person until they integrate this knowledge in a helpful manner.

Projection: This defence mechanism allows people to take unacceptable urges and emotions and attribute them to another individual. For example, a person who has the impulse to have an affair accuses their partner of cheating. Or a mother who feels she never achieved her dream pushes her child to succeed. Often, projection results in strong emotions with people pushing their projections to a disproportionate level. Thus, it tends to impact relationships and cause conflict that can only be de-escalated by uncovering acceptable urges and dealing with the resulting distress.

Acting out: This is an immature defence mechanism. It is often used by children and adolescents who are struggling. Acting out involves engaging in detrimental behaviours instead of identifying and coping with the difficult emotions underlying an issue or stressor. For example, a boy whose parents are getting divorced starts bullying classmates. Acting out takes a toll on the individual, their relationships, and their functioning in other aspects of their life, like school or work. Others are often unaware of the stressor the person is experiencing and react with anger and sadness towards the person acting out, putting a strain on the relationships or consequences of negative behaviours. Acting out distracts the person from the help, emotional support, and compassion they need and allows them to be labelled as a problem instead.

Passive aggression: This is an immature defence mechanism that significantly impacts relationships. It is used by individuals who struggle to communicate their true emotions, needs, or wants. Instead, underlying aggression and resentment are voiced in an indirect way that cannot be productively addressed.

When anger is voiced this way, the aggression hurts the intimacy and trust in a relationship, particularly if used as a pattern.

Humour: This is a mature defence mechanism. It does not distort or deny reality. Instead, a person takes uncomfortable or distressing thoughts, events, and emotions and presents them in a way that can make them feel connected to others, acknowledges feelings of futility and pain, and lead to seeking help.[140]

Sublimation: A more mature defence mechanism, sublimation takes unacceptable urges and channels them into a socially appropriate space. For example, a person with violent thoughts and fantasies writes horror books or someone who has experienced a loss starts a foundation honouring their loved one. It is considered a mature strategy because it transforms pain and distress into productive outlets and manages feelings that would disrupt society in a helpful way. These mechanisms can be explored in therapy to understand and acknowledge the underlying emotions and learn to cope with unacceptable impulses.

Unhealthy Coping Strategies

Also known as maladaptive coping strategies, these are actions to deal with distressing information, thoughts, and emotions coming into our consciousness. Instead of using healthy coping strategies, like exercise, breathing techniques, or seeking support, maladaptive coping consists of destructive behaviours, such as alcoholism, drug use, and risky sexual choices. Using coping skills, whether healthy or maladaptive, turns into a pattern that initially starts with the purposes of escape or avoidance. In case of unhealthy coping skills, this pattern of destruction causes more problems in a person's life and relationships while worsening anxiety and feelings of hopelessness around the stressor they seek to escape.

Chapter 8

Thought Distortions and Negative Thinking

'We don't see things the way we are, we see them as we are.'

—Anaïs Nin

How are negative thought patterns, blocking beliefs, lenses, and cognitive schemas developed? These are the building blocks of our perspective and views of the world, ourselves, and others. Left unexamined, the resulting narratives can lead us to live our lives in a very narrow manner without being able to consider if our views are skewed, a product of false information, or hurting us more than helping us.

We have explored the ways in which buried knowledge, trauma, and emotions shape our sense of fulfilment and quality of life through our physical and mental health. We have started to look at the mechanisms in which important knowledge is buried away from our consciousness. Now, we will look at how the issues and experiences that have shaped us along the way have created our conscious thought processes and ways of perceiving our worlds and relationships. These experiences can create positive, empowering ways of seeing our surroundings and choosing to live our lives in alignment with goals that give us meaning, fulfilment, and purpose while fostering personal growth. Whereas the negative thoughts, distorted thinking, and erroneous beliefs can result in symptoms of anxiety, depression, and distress.

Often, a person is unaware of the ways in which their thinking is distorted and struggles to accept the manner in which their beliefs and perception are disrupting their lives and well-being. These patterns of thinking and perceiving are deeply ingrained and, in most cases, have been created over a lifetime of experience in subtle and unnoticeable ways. Therapy in these situations works to examine the accuracy of beliefs and thought processes, which limit us to develop more adaptive and motivating ways of seeing our problems and experiences. At first, challenging the beliefs and ways of thinking we have taken for granted appears awkward and foreign, yet the process commonly known as cognitive behavioural therapy (CBT) results in a person growing past the ways in which their beliefs limit them. It is a way to reject unhelpful thoughts and beliefs we have inherited through legacies, trauma, and difficult situations to forge our own system of meaning-making.

CBT was created by Aaron Beck, who developed the theory that depression and other mental health issues create and exacerbate negative distortions in thinking, which give rise to negative core beliefs about an individual and their worlds. The theory is based on three aspects: negative automatic thoughts, cognitive distortions, and lastly, cognitive schemas and underlying beliefs.[141] CBT is the structured process of collaborative empiricism wherein an individual is fostered to become their own therapist by examining and evolving these three aspects of thinking into a healthier form. Through the process of CBT, the person is able to reframe and correct their own automatic negative thoughts and cognitive distortions while identifying adaptive ways to cope. This positively impacts their mental health and opens new avenues for opportunity and connection.

Aspects of the Theory Supporting CBT

Automatic negative thoughts: These are involuntary interpretations and statements resulting from our perception of an event. We do not filter or change them as they happen automatically. These thoughts often stem from our underlying beliefs and assumptions. For example, a person with the underlying belief that they are not as smart as their co-workers will have automatic thoughts stemming from this assumption. If they receive negative feedback on a project, the first thoughts they will have could be, 'I am such an idiot' or 'I will never be smart enough to do well here.' Notice that thoughts stemming from negative self-belief take a situation out of context and use it to say something critical about the individual, increasing negative feelings. Likewise, when automatic thoughts go straight to blaming someone or something else, a person misses out on the opportunity to take responsibility by accurately assessing their thoughts and actions to create change.

Cognitive distortions: These are irrational thoughts and patterns of distorting reality that cause us to interpret the world, others, and ourselves in inaccurate ways. These distortions exist in automatic thoughts and are more prevalent among people with mental illnesses such as anxiety and depression. Left unchecked, they can alienate people from others and cost them opportunities for growth. Cognitive distortions bury or hide the truth from us in a way that prevents growth and ultimately keeps us at arm's length from connection with others and achievement. There are many cognitive distortions, but some are used more frequently. We will go over them in the following section.

Common Cognitive Distortions

All or nothing thinking: Also known as black and white thinking, this is one of the most common cognitive distortions. To people with these cognitive distortions, there is no grey—a situation or experience is either at one end or the other. This often leads to individuals having low tolerance to perceived failures and setbacks. Ultimately, this way of thinking is an obstacle to achieving and sustaining goals. For example, a person who is trying to eat healthy, eats something they perceive as unhealthy. Feeling that they have broken their diet, they decide to keep eating unhealthy food until the next day. This leads to multiple days of eating the foods they perceive they will miss instead of self-correcting after the first 'unhealthy' meal and aiming for moderation. As another example, an individual feels slighted by a friend but instead of attempting to solve the issue and seeing that their friend can still be a good person despite doing a hurtful thing, they cut off the person and refuse to speak to them until they apologize.

Overgeneralization: This is another commonly employed cognitive distortion. It involves takes a singular incident and turning it into a pattern that has negative implications. The words 'always' or 'never' typically feature in these thoughts. For example, a person waitlisted for a school may think 'I am never anyone's first choice.' This kind of thought creates a defeatist attitude in the person and confirms negative false beliefs they have about themselves. At the same time, they overlook evidence to the contrary, which can disprove the pattern. The person is not conscious that they are overgeneralizing and falsely creating a pattern until they become aware of this cognitive distortion.

Catastrophizing: A person takes an event or experience and imagines its worst-case scenario. This is a common distortion that causes and maintains anxiety. For example, a person receives an elevated liver enzyme result in a blood test and assumes they have liver disease. Catastrophizing can become a frequently used distortion in all areas of someone's life, leading to an aversion to new opportunities or perceived risks. Because of its drastic negative implications, it can be accompanied by physical symptoms of anxiety, which further the person's belief that something bad will happen while leading to more catastrophic thinking.

Emotional reasoning: In this case, a person 'feels' something will happen and, thus, believes it will. Often, such cognitive distortion can be seen in events that have happened, with a person saying, 'I knew that would happen.' There are two main issues here—first, the person ignores logical reasoning and second, they only remember the times they were right but discount the times that they were not, which would disprove their feeling. For example, a person feels that they are too awkward to make new friends. When encountering new people, they do not realize that this belief makes them avoid others and appear unapproachable. When people try to speak to them, they discount these experiences and focus on times they did not feel included.

Discounting the positives: An individual only picks experiences from their past that confirm the negative pattern they have decided on. Any experiences to the contrary are discounted and not taken as proof their belief may be inaccurate. For example, if a person is trying to lose weight and, after a month of exercising and eating healthily, their weight has not decreased as much as they had aimed for. Instead of appreciating the entire picture and focusing on their clothes being looser and feeling healthier and stronger, they give up after falsely believing their actions are futile.

This distortion can be a problem while making purposeful changes, as it impacts motivation and a person's ability to accurately gauge progress. It can be detrimental to relationships as well because a person can develop an idea of their partner's issues in the relationship but be blind to the changes they are making. This pattern shows up in couples therapy—a person struggles with their partner's behaviour or trait and, due to a mix of emotional reasoning, discounting the positive, and overgeneralizing, tends to put more stock in their mistakes and less in their efforts. This can be a difficult pattern to break as many of these identified patterns and beliefs are developed and 'confirmed' over the course of the relationship and are rooted in deep emotions and dependent on the stability of the relationship.

Should statements: These are critical statements and judgments against yourself or someone else. They involve setting high standards of behaviour and experiencing guilt (towards yourself) or anger (towards others) when they are not met. Since these standards are rigid, a person does not appreciate accomplishments that are any less than the defined level. For example, 'I should have gotten an A' or 'I should not be upset about this.' When directed towards others, they can take the form of, 'My mother should know better than to message me when I am upset' or 'A person who cares about me should not act like that.' Should statements lead to unnecessarily critical and judgmental thoughts and beliefs about yourself, which lead to defence mechanisms burying important knowledge and emotions. Ultimately, this causes feelings of low self-worth and psychiatric symptoms. In relationships, should statements deny a person's accountability and are an unnecessarily pessimistic view of another's actions.

Personalization: This involves taking the blame or assigning blame for something negative that was out of your control. A common example is assuming that a person is acting in a more reserved or irritated manner because of something you have done even when there is no evidence that suggests so. This leads to feelings of guilt and resentment and, often, to someone becoming the problem in an attempt to fix it. Some people, like children of abusers or addicts, or people pleasers, learn to be sensitive to changes in other's moods to make peace and de-escalate conflict. The issue here is that personalization is an inaccurate analysis of the situation that over assigns responsibility to one person or blame to another person. The focus becomes the conflict and guilt or anger which ensues instead of solving the problem or letting go of the issue when appropriate.

Ways to Cope with Cognitive Distortions

1. Stay in the present. Focus on the situation at hand without extrapolating its meaning.
2. When upset, write down the situation and your specific thoughts. Now, write down your related emotions. Ask yourself if your thoughts have any cognitive distortions in them. A tip to identify if your thoughts are distorted is when they include polarizing words like 'should', 'never', and 'always', or if they attack your or another person's personality and self-worth. Ask yourself how you can look at the situation in a healthier and more productive way. A good way to do this at the beginning is by using a thought log. You can use the one provided in this book to get started.
3. Frequently ask yourself if you are looking at the situation accurately when you experience negative thoughts. Ask yourself what evidence supports these negative thoughts. What evidence does not?
4. If you find yourself overthinking and ruminating, it is likely due to cognitive distortions. Write your thoughts down in the thought log and participate in an activity to reduce anxiety. This could mean going for a walk, speaking to a friend (about other things), or taking a bath. Once you are feeling calmer, return to your thought log and re-evaluate the accuracy of your thoughts.
5. Avoid absolutes and labels. These are key signs of cognitive distortions that lead to negative, defeatist thinking.

Let's now take a look at the cognitive schemas and core beliefs that lead to automatic negative thoughts and cognitive distortions.

Cognitive Schemas

Schemas are defined as the 'basic structural components of cognitive organization through which humans come to identify, interpret, categorize, and evaluate their experiences'.[142] Essentially, they are shortcuts created to interpret and organize information. They have protective value because they stop us from feeling overwhelmed and overstimulated by new experiences. They are in line with our needs as a species to quickly make meaning of and organize information.

There are four main types of cognitive schemas:

1. Person schemas: This encompasses your mental framework for yourself and other individuals. It can include templates of the traits and behaviours you expect from a specific friend or of what a friend is in general. If a friend behaves in a new way, we attempt to fit this in with our experience of the person and find an explanation, which feels familiar and reassuring. If a friend starts consistently behaving differently from our schema of them, we begin to worry about them or jump to the conclusion that they are no longer interested in our relationship. Stereotypes are examples of person schemas that lead to us over assuming negative characteristics about people and subsequent discrimination.
2. Social or role schemas: These include ways of organizing social norms, cues, and behaviours. They are scripts for how people behave in certain situations such as at a football game or when dating someone.
3. Self-schemas: Your self-schema includes core beliefs, values, standards, behaviours, and goals that you identify with who you are. This schema evolves over your lifetime, with more becoming conscious with age.

4. Event schemas: These schemas explain what to do at certain events such a birthday or during Christmas. Developing an event schema allows a person to feel more comfortable when entering a new situation, as they feel accustomed to the rules and behaviours expected of them.

As you can imagine, schemas can have a positive or negative impact on someone's life. A schema is positive when it offers protection and comfort to an individual. But, to be beneficial, individuals must leave room for schemas to evolve and be open to change. There are schemas underlying depression, anxiety, and other mental health issues, along with determining our sense of self-worth and confidence. These negative schemas only allow information that supports the negative belief (like, 'I am worthless') to be gathered but disqualify information that contradicts an erroneous belief.

When we use CBT in therapy or a person begins their own quest to change their thinking, our first step is to identify which schemas and core beliefs are being triggered in their situation. We get this information by identifying their automatic negative thoughts and cognitive distortions and tracing them back to the underlying belief. For example, a person with a core belief 'no one will ever choose me' has negative thoughts and distort their thinking in a way that affirms this belief. This is reflected in multiple facets of their life such as their family dynamics, work life, and attempts at forming relationships. A belief such as 'no one will ever choose me' is likely to be born through early childhood dynamics and attachment issues. From there, it holds a place in people's minds at an unconscious level, with new experiences reaffirming that they are not special or worthy enough to be chosen being collected as proof. This changes the way the person acts with others and what they accept and do not expect for themselves.

The first step to addressing this form of thinking is bringing this information to consciousness by recognizing patterns in an individual's automatic negative thoughts. When the negative core beliefs are brought to light, a person is taught to recognize that these schemas and beliefs are erroneous. The person must undergo a learning process of challenging and reframing thoughts. Once they do this, they quickly begin to realize the ways in which their erroneous beliefs and distortions have limited their lives and potential. This makes way for choosing a more empowering and healthy way of thinking, overcoming system of beliefs and schemas, and allowing growth and finding meaning and fulfilment.

This process does not have to be undertaken alone. Psychologists and other therapists are well trained guides to help you understand how you can evolve your thinking patterns while injecting hope and strength into the process. While starting off as a guide and facilitator, the process of facing and evolving our thoughts and beliefs leads to us being able to act as our own therapists.

Chapter 9

An Examined Life: Embracing the Life We Bury

> 'An unexamined life is not worth living.'
>
> —Socrates

Socrates, who was once considered to be the wisest man in ancient Greece, argued that introspection about our lives paves the way to a meaningful and purposeful existence. Without examining our lives, he insisted, we would be 'no different from mere beasts', focusing on surface pleasures and survival without greater fulfilment. Socrates' idea of meaning and purpose differs from the one encouraged in this book. For him, the purpose of life was morality and virtue. This book argues for a much more varied definition of meaning, purpose, and fulfilment, which is dependent on the values and beliefs consciously chosen by an individual.

One person's idea of fulfilment and purpose may involve living their lives with dignity and using their voice when needed; another person's may be to stay connected to their family, while someone else's may be to live a simple life of appreciation. The parameters and standards of fulfilment and meaning are up to you and involve creating a system that allows you to feel motivated to progress towards your goals without feeling stuck.

One of the most common reasons people seek therapy is because they feel unfulfilled, unmotivated, and do not know where to find meaning in their lives. Usually, this state of dissatisfaction and inertia manifests in symptoms of anxiety or depression and difficulties with sleep, motivation, and engagement. Other times, people comes with difficulties connecting with others and sustaining relationships or experiencing symptoms of PTSD surrounding an unprocessed history of abuse or neglect. In both examples, their unfulfillment is signified by psychiatric symptoms and the key is to uncover the buried and unacknowledged information and emotions that are making them feel stuck.

Let us look at the first situation, when someone comes to therapy feeling unmotivated and unfulfilled. When Tia came to see me, she was a twenty-eight-year-old woman who complained of burnout and feeling unfulfilled at her job and in her relationships. Tia was an IT consultant who had been in her role for two years, having moved to Malaysia to start this job. Originally from France, Tia had to start anew, making friends and dating when, in the past, her relationships had begun naturally, in school and college.

Tia was someone who approached new opportunities and experiences with excitement and focused on the potential before her. She thrived on energy and engagement with others and, as a result, her mood could vary depending on the situation and people she was surrounded by. Her conscious focus was on her dissatisfaction with her job and company. Tia was mildly aware of her general lack of fulfilment, but her feelings of anxiety and emotional exhaustion quickly stopped her from delving further. Once we started working on her anxiety, it became clear that underneath her symptoms, she felt like she was neither making the deep connections she was looking for nor challenging herself enough at work and in her life. Tia had decompartmentalized and dissociated important knowledge from her awareness. She shared she had a boyfriend of two years whom she did not speak about. It was as though she would disconnect him from her conscious awareness when she was not with him.

In the first discussion, Tia stated in (unenthusiastic) terms that her relationship was all right, and her partner was a good person. It took weeks of Tia feeling safe in the therapeutic relationship for her to disclose that she had a history of relationships in which she faced controlling behaviour and had trouble voicing her own needs. Tia had never processed these relationships in therapy and felt unsure of herself, feeling that she was exaggerating the difficulties she faced and worried that she was too demanding or picky. When exploring the roots of Tia's negative core beliefs that she was 'too much' and 'was not a good partner', we brought to light that Tia's father had (and was) extremely narcissistic. From a young age, Tia had been taught to meet her father's expectations for her and to value what he valued for her in life. His affection and attention were conditioned on Tia being compliant with his goals. This also meant putting up with his unstable moods and bolstering his lack of self-worth.

To address the core of Tia's sense of unfulfillment and unhappiness, and to help her connect meaningfully, we brought to light these patterns and the disconnected emotions she had towards herself and her current relationship. It became clear that she was holding herself back from asserting herself, acknowledging flaws in her relationship, and trusting her judgment.

Due to Tia's inquisitive and insightful nature, she worked hard to understand the knowledge she had buried. She came to understand the generational patterns of narcissistic abuse her family had endured, the emotional toll of the relationships she had experienced, and the impact this had on her choice of men who perpetuated this pattern. She learned the role she had played in maintaining these dynamics, as well as how she had directed her life towards the goals her parents had chosen for her and encouraged her to live by. She was able to rethink what she wanted out of her life and relationships. This led to her breaking up with her boyfriend, who perpetuated the feelings of guilt and shame she felt about herself because she could not feel happy with him. She also left her job to start her own business. While both were difficult endeavours, Tia recognized the strengths that made her successful and used them to motivate herself. She was also able to challenge and reconsider negative thought patterns and defence mechanisms that kept her stuck in a dissatisfied place.

In all, I saw Tia for about a year and during that time, her confidence about who she was and her acceptance of her wants and needs increased dramatically. Additionally, she was able to understand the unhelpful and destructive behaviours and thought processes that were contributing to her responsibility in both her friendships and relationships.

Like Tia, here's a roadmap for you of the elements you must explore to lead an examined life. These are:

1. Epigenetics: What experiences have your ancestors had that have modified the blueprint of your genetics?
2. Intergenerational trauma: How does collective, historical, and generational trauma live on in your family? How have the stories shared shaped lessons on safety, agency, and empowerment?
3. Attachment: What is your attachment style? How has it impacted the partners you have chosen? How has it impacted your trust in yourself and others?
4. Trauma and psychological distress: What experiences have you been through that have negatively impacted you? How are they holding you back? How can you empower yourself to live the life you want?
5. Family dynamics: What is your birth order? What are the legacies you have inherited from your family? What values do you want to live by? What narratives are important for you going forward?

6. Defence mechanisms and maladaptive coping: How have you kept the difficult knowledge that has been passed down to you and associated emotions out of your consciousness? What defence mechanisms do you use? How can you develop healthy and active ways of coping when you feel distressed?
7. Thought distortions, negative thinking, and cognitive schemas: What are your core beliefs and schemas? What cognitive distortions and automatic negative thoughts do you have as a result? What will you do to take responsibility for the accuracy of your thoughts and commit to reframing as healthy thoughts and processes?

While the weight of your history and experiences may feel heavy, they do not have to be the albatross around your neck that prevents you from living the life you want. Using defence mechanisms, distortions, or maladaptive coping strategies like avoidance, you give power to the aspects of your inheritance that can hurt you. Interestingly, we use these strategies out of attempts to protect ourselves, but at a cost. We believe that we cannot handle the whole truth and weight of all of our knowledge, emotions, and thoughts. While these mechanisms and coping strategies aid us in finding temporary relief and carrying on through our days, this comes at the expense of trusting ourselves and those who support us to handle the whole truth of ourselves. If, instead, we would allow ourselves to gradually examine the stories, emotions, and knowledge passed through the generations of our families that evolve through our lives, we would simultaneously build our trust and connection to ourselves.

These experiences are not to be feared. They are your blueprint to evolving and determining your own potential. This process is within your control. You can start and stop, breathe and rest, and at other times, be propelled forward by the courage and knowledge you find in yourself. Have hope and solace by recognizing that examining the difficulties you have faced is the answer to finding the fulfilment and relief you are looking for. You are not alone in doing so. I hope you will take the first steps towards embracing your full glory, guided by this book and with the support of those around you.

Acknowledgments

I am grateful to the generations before me who have illuminated the importance of understanding where we came from and how we are shaped. I find happiness in seeing the seeds that were planted, which continue to grow in my children as I watch them flourish. Without my parents and grandparents and the openness and curiosity they encouraged me to have, I would never have had the experiences and opportunities I have now. I am lucky to have been exposed to so many different people from so many different places and to have had a place in their lives. I am thankful for my friends who have made each place I have lived in feel like home and for continuing to be a part of who I am, even if we no longer live in the same place.

To my parents, you have given me opportunities and believed in my ideas, thank you for entertaining this path I have followed. Thank you for tirelessly helping me.

I could not have had the words to put together this book without the belief and investment of the mentors I have had along the way. Of these, none have been more influential than those I met during my time at Edward M. Kennedy Community Health Center, where I truly learned about dissociation and trauma, and began a lifelong interest in those who struggled with them. Laurie Costigan and Sarah Katz, thank you for patiently guiding me.

To my clients, you have brought my training and knowledge to life. No one has taught me better than the experiences I have had while humbly working with you.

Last but never the least, thank you to my children and husband. I am always thinking of how to make our family the most it can be. I could not have done this without you, Mike. I will always remember writing this book while pregnant with August, and the love and support from you, Violet, and Quinn. You all are the brightest part of my day and my hope for the future.

Endnotes

1 Thumfart, K.M., Jawaid, A.., Bright, K.., Flachsmann, M., Mansuy, I.M. (2022). Epigenetics of Childhood Trauma: Long Term Sequelae and Potential for Treatment. *Neuroscience & Biobehavioral Reviews*, 132, 1049–1066. https://doi.org/10.1016/j.neubiorev.2021.10.042.

2 Burton, N.O., Greer, E.L. (2021). Multigenerational Epigenetic Inheritance: Transmitting Information Across Generations. *Semin Cell Dev Biol*, 127, 121–132. doi: 10.1016/j.semcdb.2021.08.006. PMID: 34426067; PMCID: PMC8858334.

3 Yehuda, R., Lehrner, A. (2018). Intergenerational Transmission of Trauma Effects: Putative Role of Epigenetic Mechanisms. *World Psychiatry*, 17(3), 243–257. doi: 10.1002/wps.20568. PMID: 30192087; PMCID: PMC6127768.

4 Kellermann, N.P. (2013). Epigenetic Transmission of Holocaust Trauma: Can Nightmares Be Inherited?. *The Israel Journal of Psychiatry and Related Sciences*, 50(1), 33–39.

5 Kessler, R.C., Aguilar-Gaxiola, S., Alonso, J., Benjet, C., Bromet, E.J., Cardoso, G., et al. (2017). Trauma and PTSD in the WHO World Mental Health Surveys. *Eur J Psychotraumatol*, 8(sup5), 1353383. doi:10.1080/20008198.2017.1353383

6 Yehuda, R. (2022). Trauma in the Family Tree. Scientific American Publisher; Wolynn, M. (2016). *It Didn't Start with You: How Inherited Family Trauma Shapes Who We Are and How to End the Cycle*. New York: Viking.

7 Yehuda, R., Lehrner, A. (2018). Intergenerational Transmission of Trauma Effects: Putative Role of Epigenetic Mechanisms. *World Psychiatry*, 17(3), 243–257. doi: 10.1002/wps.20568. PMID: 30192087; PMCID: PMC6127768.
8 Kellermann, N.P. (2013). Epigenetic Transmission of Holocaust Trauma: Can Nightmares Be Inherited?. *The Israel Journal of Psychiatry and Related Sciences*, 50(1), 33–39.
9 Ibid.
10 Silver, R.C. (2002). Nationwide Longitudinal Study of Psychological Responses to September 11. *JAMA*, 288(10), 1235. https://doi.org/10.1001/jama.288.10.1235
11 Burton, N.O., Greer, E.L. (2021). Multigenerational Epigenetic Inheritance: Transmitting Information Across Generations. *Semin Cell Dev Biol*, 127, 121–132. doi: 10.1016/j.semcdb.2021.08.006. PMID: 34426067; PMCID: PMC8858334.
12 Yehuda, R., Lehrner, A. (2018). Intergenerational Transmission of Trauma Effects: Putative Role of Epigenetic Mechanisms. *World Psychiatry*, 17(3), 243–257. doi: 10.1002/wps.20568. PMID: 30192087; PMCID: PMC6127768.
13 Thumfart, K.M., Jawaid, A.., Bright, K.., Flachsmann, M., Mansuy, I.M. (2022). Epigenetics of Childhood Trauma: Long Term Sequelae and Potential for Treatment. *Neuroscience & Biobehavioral Reviews*, 132, 1049–1066, https://doi.org/10.1016/j.neubiorev.2021.10.042.; Švorcová, J. (2023). Transgenerational Epigenetic Inheritance of Traumatic Experience in Mammals. *Genes (Basel)*, 14(1), 120. doi: 10.3390/genes14010120. PMID: 36672861; PMCID: PMC9859285.
14 Kellermann, N.P. (2013). Epigenetic Transmission of Holocaust Trauma: Can Nightmares Be Inherited?. *The Israel Journal of Psychiatry and Related Sciences*, 50(1), 33–39.
15 Ibid.

16 Rodriguez, L., Gomez, M. M., Kaiser, L., Horowitz, M., Johns, M., de la Torre, A. (2015). The Drought's Effect on Food Security among Farm Workers. *Journal of Nutrition Education and Behavior*, 47(4). https://doi.org/10.1016/j.jneb.2015.04.274.

17 Serpeloni, F., Nätt, D., Assis, S. G., Wieling, E., Elbert, T. (2019). Experiencing Community and Domestic Violence Is Associated with Epigenetic Changes in DNA Methylation of BDNF and CLPX in Adolescents. *Psychophysiology*, 57(1). https://doi.org/10.1111/psyp.13382.

18 Bick, J., Naumova, O., Hunter, S., Barbot, B., Lee, M., Luthar, S.S., Raefski, A., Grigorenko, E.L. (2012). Childhood Adversity and DNA Methylation of Genes Involved in the Hypothalamus-Pituitary-Adrenal Axis and Immune System: Whole-Genome and Candidate-Gene Associations. *Dev Psychopathol*, 24(4), 1417-25. doi: 10.1017/S0954579412000806. PMID: 23062307; PMCID: PMC3755948.

19 Sultan, F.A., Day, J.J. (2011). Epigenetic Mechanisms in Memory and Synaptic Function. *Epigenomics*, 3(2), 157–81. doi: 10.2217/epi.11.6. PMID: 22122279; PMCID: PMC3350307; Komar-Fletcher, M., Wojas, J., Rutkowska, M., Raczyńska, G., Nowacka, A., Jurek, J.M. (2023) Negative Environmental Influences on the Developing Brain Mediated by Epigenetic Modifications. *Explor Neurosci*, 2, 193–211. https://doi.org/10.37349/en.2023.00021

20 Vidrascu, E.M., Bashore, A.C., Howard, T.D., Moore, J.B. (2019). Effects of Early- and Mid-Life Stress on DNA Methylation of Genes Associated with Subclinical Cardiovascular Disease and Cognitive Impairment: A Systematic Review. *BMC Med Genet*, 20, 39. https://doi.org/10.1186/s12881-019-0764-4

21 García-Moreno, C.., Pallitto, C. (2013). *Global and Regional Estimates of Violence Against Women: Prevalence and Health Effects of Intimate Partner Violence and Nonpartner*

Sexual Violence. Geneva: WHO. https://iris.who.int/bitstream/handle/10665/85239/9789241564625_eng.pdf?sequence=1; Claudia García-Moreno, LynnMarie Sardinha. (2018). *Violence Against Women Prevalence Estimates, 2018*. Geneva: WHO. https://iris.who.int/bitstream/handle/10665/341337/9789240022256-eng.pdf?sequence=1.

22 Radtke, K.M., Ruf, M., Gunter, H.M., Dohrmann, K., Schauer, M., Meyer, A., & Elbert, T. (2011). Transgenerational Impact of Intimate Partner Violence on Methylation in the Promoter of the Glucocorticoid Receptor. *Translational Psychiatry*, 1(7). https://doi.org/10.1038/tp.2011.21

23 Labonté, B., Azoulay, N., Yerko, V., Turecki, G., Brunet, A. (2014). Epigenetic Modulation of Glucocorticoid Receptors in Posttraumatic Stress Disorder. *Translational Psychiatry*, 4(3), e368. doi: 10.1038/tp.2014.3. PMID: 24594779; PMCID: PMC3966043.

24 Piccinini, A., Bailo, P., Barbara, G., Miozzo, M., Tabano, S., Colapietro, P. et al. (2023). Violence Against Women and Stress-related Disorders: Seeking for Associated Epigenetic Signatures, a Pilot Study. *Healthcare*, 11(2), 173. doi:10.3390/healthcare11020173

25 Radtke, K.M., Ruf, M., Gunter, H.M., Dohrmann, K., Schauer, M., Meyer, A., & Elbert, T. (2011). Transgenerational Impact of Intimate Partner Violence on Methylation in the Promoter of the Glucocorticoid Receptor. *Translational Psychiatry*, 1(7). https://doi.org/10.1038/tp.2011.21

26 Piccinini, A., Bailo, P., Barbara, G., Miozzo, M., Tabano, S., Colapietro, P. et al. (2023). Violence Against Women and Stress-related Disorders: Seeking for Associated Epigenetic Signatures, a Pilot Study. *Healthcare*, 11(2), 173. doi:10.3390/healthcare11020173

27 Rodriguez, L., Gomez, M. M., Kaiser, L., Horowitz, M., Johns, M., de la Torre, A. (2015). The Drought's Effect on Food Security among Farm Workers. *Journal of Nutrition*

    Education and Behavior, 47(4). https://doi.org/10.1016/j.jneb.2015.04.274.

28 Dion, A., Muñoz, P.T., Franklin, T.B. (2022). Epigenetic Mechanisms Impacted by Chronic Stress across the Rodent Lifespan. *Neurobiol Stress*, 17, 100434. doi: 10.1016/j.ynstr.2022.100434. PMID: 35198660; PMCID: PMC8841894.

29 Trauma, APA Dictionary of Psychology. (n.d.). American Psychological Association. https://dictionary.apa.org/trauma

30 Harvard Medical School, 2007. National Comorbidity Survey (NCS). (2017, August 21). https://www.hcp.med.harvard.edu/ncs/index.php.

31 Bahari, R., Mohamad Alwi, M.N., Ahmad, M.R., Mohd Saiboon, I. (2017). Incidence and Demographical Characteristics of Patients with Post-Traumatic Stress Disorder due to Motor Vehicle Accidents. *Malaysian Family Physician: The Official Journal of the Academy of Family Physicians of Malaysia*, 12(3), 2–7.

32 Burton, N.O., Greer, E.L. (2021). Multigenerational Epigenetic Inheritance: Transmitting Information Across Generations. *Semin Cell Dev Biol*, 127, 121–132. doi: 10.1016/j.semcdb.2021.08.006. PMID: 34426067; PMCID: PMC8858334.

33 Kinzie, J.D., Boehnlein, J.K., Leung, P.K., Moore, L.J., Riley, C., Smith, D. (1990). The Prevalence of Posttraumatic Stress Disorder and Its Clinical Significance among Southeast Asian Refugees. *American Journal of Psychiatry*, 147, 913–917.

34 Coenen, P., van der Molen, H.F. (2021). What Work-Related Exposures Are Associated with Post-Traumatic Stress Disorder? A Systematic Review with Meta-Analysis. *BMJ Open*, 11(8), e049651. doi: 10.1136/bmjopen-2021-049651. PMID: 34433603; PMCID: PMC8388294.

35 Intergenerational Trauma. APA Dictionary of Psychology. (n.d.). American Psychological Association. https://dictionary.apa.org/intergenerational-trauma

36 Danieli, Y., Norris, F.H., Engdahl, B. (2016). Multigenerational Legacies of Trauma: Modeling the What and How of Transmission. *American Journal of Orthopsychiatry*, 86(6), 639–651. https://doi.org/10.1037/ort0000145

37 Schultz, K., Cattaneo, L., Sabina, C., Brunner, L., Jackson, S., Serrata, J. (2016). Key Roles of Community Connectedness in Healing from Trauma. *Psychology of Violence*, 6, 42–48. doi:10.1037/vio0000025.

38 Solomon, Z., Mikulincer, M., Avitzur, E. (1988). Coping, Locus of Control, Social Support, and Combat-Related Posttraumatic Stress Disorder: A Prospective Study. *Journal of Personality and Social Psychology*, 55(2), 279–285. https://doi.org/10.1037//0022-3514.55.2.279.

39 Rodriguez, L., Gomez, M. M., Kaiser, L., Horowitz, M., Johns, M., de la Torre, A. (2015). The Drought's Effect on Food Security among Farm Workers. *Journal of Nutrition Education and Behavior*, 47(4). https://doi.org/10.1016/j.jneb.2015.04.274.

40 Bick, J., Naumova, O., Hunter, S., Barbot, B., Lee, M., Luthar, S.S., Raefski, A., Grigorenko, E.L. (2012). Childhood Adversity and DNA Methylation of Genes Involved in the Hypothalamus-Pituitary-Adrenal Axis and Immune System: Whole-Genome and Candidate-Gene Associations. *Dev Psychopathol*, 24(4), 1417-25. doi: 10.1017/S0954579412000806. PMID: 23062307; PMCID: PMC3755948.

41 Serpeloni, F., Nätt, D., Assis, S. G., Wieling, E., Elbert, T. (2019). Experiencing Community and Domestic Violence Is Associated with Epigenetic Changes in DNA Methylation of BDNF and CLPX in Adolescents. *Psychophysiology*, 57(1). https://doi.org/10.1111/psyp.13382

42 Danieli, Y., Norris, F., Lindert, J., Paisner, V., Engdahl, B., Richter, J. (2015). The Danieli Inventory of Multigenerational Legacies of Trauma, Part I: Survivors' Posttrauma Adaptational

Styles in their Children's Eyes. *Journal of Psychiatric Research*, 68. doi: 10.1016/j.jpsychires.2015.06.011.
43 Danieli, Y. (1998). Justice and Reparation: Steps in the Process of Healing, in Christopher C. Joyner (ed.), *Reining in Impunity for International Crimes and Serious Violations of Fundamental Human Rights: Proceedings of the Siracusa Conference 17–21 September 1998*. 303–312.
44 Danieli, Y., Norris, F., Muller-Paisner, V., Kronenberg, S., Richter, J. (2015). The Danieli Inventory of Multigenerational Legacies of Trauma, Part II: Reparative Adaptational Impacts. *American Journal of Orthopsychiatry*, 85(3), 229–237; Dekel, R., Goldblatt, H. (2008). Is There Intergenerational Transmission of Trauma? The Case of Combat Veterans' Children. *American Journal of Orthopsychiatry*, 78(3), 281–289. https://doi.org/10.1037/a0013955
45 Menzies, K. (2019). Understanding the Australian Aboriginal Experience of Collective, Historical and Intergenerational Trauma. *International Social Work*, 62(6), 1522–1534. https://doi.org/10.1177/0020872819870585
46 Menzies, P. (2010). Intergenerational Trauma from a Mental Health Perspective. *Native Social Work Journal*, 7, 63–85.
47 Quayle, A.F., Sonn C.C. (2019). Amplifying the Voices of Indigenous Elders through Community Arts and Narrative Inquiry: Stories of Oppression, Psychosocial Suffering, and Survival. *Am J Community Psychol*, 64(1–2), 46–58. doi: 10.1002/ajcp.12367. Epub 2019 Jul 31. PMID: 31365131; PMCID: PMC6772144.
48 Ibid.
49 Vidrascu, E.M., Bashore, A.C., Howard, T.D., Moore, J.B (2019). Effects of Early- and Mid-Life Stress on DNA Methylation of Genes Associated with Subclinical Cardiovascular Disease and Cognitive Impairment: A

Systematic Review. *BMC Med Genet*, 20, 39. https://doi.org/10.1186/s12881-019-0764-4

50 Komar-Fletcher, M., Wojas, J., Rutkowska, M., Raczyńska, G., Nowacka, A., Jurek, J.M. (2023). Negative Environmental Influences on the Developing Brain Mediated by Epigenetic Modifications. *Explor Neurosci*, 2, 193–211. https://doi.org/10.37349/en.2023.00021

51 Blue Bird Jernigan, V., D'Amico, E.J., Duran, B., Buchwald, D. (2020). Multilevel and Community-Level Interventions with Native Americans: Challenges and Opportunities. *Prev Sci*, 21(Suppl 1), 65–73. doi: 10.1007/s11121-018-0916-3. PMID: 29860640; PMCID: PMC6275139.

52 Bezo, B., Maggi, S. (2015). Living In "Survival Mode:" Intergenerational Transmission of Trauma from the Holodomor Genocide of 1932–1933 in Ukraine. *Soc Sci Med*, 134, 87–94. doi: 10.1016/j.socscimed.2015.04.009. PMID: 25931287.

53 About Adverse Childhood Experiences. (2024, 16 May). Adverse Childhood Experiences (ACEs), U.S. Centers for Disease Control and Prevention. https://www.cdc.gov/violenceprevention/aces/index.html

54 Ibid.

55 Ibid.

56 Hussaini, K.S., Powell, T.O., Christensen, M., Woodall, L. (2016). The Impact of Adverse Childhood Experiences (ACE) on Health-Related Quality of Life, Mental Health, and Hospitalizations in Delaware. *Dela J Public Health*, 2(5), 54–57. doi: 10.32481/djph.2016.12.017. PMID: 34466886; PMCID: PMC8389792.

57 Schickedanz, A., Halfon, N., Sastry, N., Chung, P.J. (2018). Parents' Adverse Childhood Experiences and Their Children's Behavioral Health Problems. *Pediatrics*, 142(2), e20180023. doi:

10.1542/peds.2018-0023. Epub 2018 Jul 9. PMID: 29987168; PMCID: PMC6317990.
58 Breiding, M.J., Basile, K.C., Smith, S.G., Black, M.C., Mahendra, R.R. (2015). *Intimate Partner Violence Surveillance: Uniform Definitions and Recommended Data Elements, Version 2.0.* Atlanta: National Center for Injury Prevention and Control, Centers for Disease Control and Prevention.
59 Felitti, V.J., Anda, R.F., Nordenberg, D., Williamson, D.F., Spitz, A.M., Edwards, V., Koss, M.P., Marks, J.S. (1998). Relationship of Childhood Abuse and Household Dysfunction to Many of the Leading Causes of Death in Adults, The Adverse Childhood Experiences (ACE) Study. *American Journal of Preventive Medicine*, 14(4), 245–258. https://doi.org/10.1016/s0749-3797(98)00017-8
60 Global and Regional Estimates of Violence Against Women. (n.d.). World Health Organization. https://www.who.int/publications/i/item/9789241564625
61 Montalvo-Liendo, N., Fredland, N., McFarlane, J., Lui, F., Koci, A.F., Nava, A. (2015). The Intersection of Partner Violence and Adverse Childhood Experiences: Implications for Research and Clinical Practice. *Issues in Mental Health Nursing*, 36(12), 989–1006. https://doi.org/10.3109/01612840.2015.1074767
62 Forke, C.M., Catallozzi, M., Localio, A.R., Grisso, J.A., Wiebe, D.J., Fein, J.A. (2019), Intergenerational Effects of Witnessing Domestic Violence: Health of the Witnesses and Their Children. *Preventive Medicine Reports*, 15, 100942. doi: 10.1016/j.pmedr.2019.100942. PMID: 31321205; PMCID: PMC6614529.
63 Meyer, S., Reeves, E., Fitz-Gibbon, K. (2021). The Intergenerational Transmission of Family Violence: Mothers'

Perceptions of Children's Experiences and Use of Violence in the Home. *Child & Family Social Work*, 26(3), 476–484. https://doi.org/10.1111/cfs.12830

64 Lünnemann, M.K.M., Horst, F.C.P.V., Prinzie, P., Luijk, M.P.C.M., Steketee, M. (2019). The Intergenerational Impact of Trauma and Family Violence on Parents and Their Children. *Child Abuse & Neglect*, 96, 104134. https://doi.org/10.1016/j.chiabu.2019.104134

65 Kitzmann, K.M., Gaylord, N.K., Holt, A.R., & Kenny, E.D. (2003). Child Witnesses to Domestic Violence: A Meta-analytic Review. *Journal of Consulting and Clinical Psychology*, 71(2), 339–352. https://doi.org/10.1037/0022-006x.71.2.339

66 Bowlby, J. (1988). *A Secure Base: Parent-Child Attachment and Healthy Human Development*. Basic Books.

67 Ibid.

68 Collins, N.L. (1996). Revised Adult Attachment Scale (RAAS) [Database record]. APA PsycTests. https://doi.org/10.1037/t19162-000

69 Secure Attachment, APA Dictionary of Psychology. (n.d.). American Psychological Association. https://dictionary.apa.org/secure-attachment

70 Insecure Attachment, APA Dictionary of Psychology. (n.d.). American Psychological Association. https://dictionary.apa.org/insecure-attachment

71 Avoidant Attachment, APA Dictionary of Psychology. (n.d.). American Psychological Association. https://dictionary.apa.org/avoidant-attachment

72 Disorganized Attachment, APA Dictionary of Psychology. (n.d.). American Psychological Association. https://dictionary.apa.org/disorganized-attachment

73 Stackert, R.A. (2003). Why Am I Unsatisfied? Adult Attachment Style, Gendered Irrational Relationship Beliefs,

and Young Adult Romantic Relationship Satisfaction. *Personality and Individual Differences,* 34(8), 1419–1429.
74 Ibid.
75 Repetition Compulsion, APA Dictionary of Psychology. (n.d.). American Psychological Association. https://dictionary.apa.org/repetition-compulsion
76 Trauma. (n.d.). Cambridge Free English Dictionary. https://dictionary.cambridge.org/dictionary/english/trauma
77 Trauma Types. (n.d.). The National Child Traumatic Stress Network. https://www.nctsn.org/what-is-child-trauma/trauma-types
78 American Psychiatric Association. (2022). *Diagnostic and Statistical Manual of Mental Disorders: DSM-5-TR.* American Psychiatric Association Publishing.
79 Benjet, C., Bromet, E., Karam, E.G., Kessler, R.C., McLaughlin, K.A., Ruscio, A.M., Shahly, V., et al. (2015). The Epidemiology of Traumatic Event Exposure Worldwide: Results from the World Mental Health Survey Consortium. *Psychological Medicine,* 46(2), 327–343. https://doi.org/10.1017/s0033291715001981
80 Ibid.
81 Schultz, K., Cattaneo, L., Sabina, C., Brunner, L., Jackson, S., Serrata, J. (2016). Key Roles of Community Connectedness in Healing from Trauma. *Psychology of Violence,* 6, 42–48. doi: 10.1037/vio0000025.
82 de Bellis, M.D., Zisk, A. (2014). The Biological Effects of Childhood Trauma. *Child and Adolescent Psychiatric Clinics of North America,* 23(2), 185–222. https://doi.org/10.1016/j.chc.2014.01.002
83 How Trauma Is Changing Children's Brains. (2010). National Education Association. https://www.nea.org/nea-today/all-news-articles/how-trauma-changing-childrens-brains

84 Jeon, H.J., Suh, T., Lee, H.J., Hahm, B.J., Lee, J.Y., Cho, S.J., Lee, Y.R. et al. (2007). Partial Versus Full PTSD in the Korean Community: Prevalence, Duration, Correlates, Comorbidity, and Dysfunctions. *Depression and Anxiety*, 24(8), 577–585. https://doi.org/10.1002/da.20270

85 Karam, E.G., Mneimneh, Z.N., Dimassi, H., Fayyad, J.A., Karam, A.N., Nasser, S.C. et al. (2008). Lifetime Prevalence of Mental Disorders in Lebanon: First Onset, Treatment, and Exposure to War. *PLoS Medicine*, 5(4). doi:10.1371/journal.pmed.0050061

86 Benjet, C., Bromet, E., Karam, E.G., Kessler, R.C., McLaughlin, K.A., Ruscio, A.M., Shahly, V. et al. (2015). The Epidemiology of Traumatic Event Exposure Worldwide: Results from the World Mental Health Survey Consortium. *Psychological Medicine*, 46(2), 327–343. https://doi.org/10.1017/s0033291715001981

87 de Bellis, M.D., Zisk, A. (2014). The Biological Effects of Childhood Trauma. *Child and Adolescent Psychiatric Clinics of North America*, 23(2), 185–222. https://doi.org/10.1016/j.chc.2014.01.002

88 American Psychiatric Association. (2013). *Diagnostic and Statistical Manual of Mental Disorders* (5th ed.). American Psychiatric Association Publishing. https://doi.org/10.1176/appi.books.9780890425596

89 Katrinli, S., Oliveira, N.C.S., Felger, J.C., Michopoulos, V., Smith, A.K. (2022, August 4). The Role of the Immune System in Posttraumatic Stress Disorder. Nature News. https://www.nature.com/articles/s41398-022-02094-7#citeas

90 Hsu, T.W., Bai, Y.M., Tsai, S.J., Chen, T.J., Chen, M.H., Liang, C.S. (2024). Risk of Autoimmune Diseases After Post-Traumatic Stress Disorder: A Nationwide Cohort Study.

European Archives of Psychiatry and Clinical Neuroscience, 274(3), 487–495. doi:10.1007/s00406-023-01639-1

91 Katrinli, S., Oliveira, N.C.S., Felger, J.C., Michopoulos, V., Smith, A.K. (2022, August 4). The Role of the Immune System in Posttraumatic Stress Disorder. Nature News. https://www.nature.com/articles/s41398-022-02094-7#citeas

92 Bennett, J.M., Reeves, G., Billman, G.E., Sturmberg, J.P. (2018). Inflammation–Nature's Way to Efficiently Respond to All Types of Challenges: Implications for Understanding and Managing "the Epidemic" of Chronic Diseases. *Front Med*, 5, 316. doi: 10.3389/fmed.2018.00316. Duan, L., Rao, X., Sigdel, K.R. (2019). Regulation of Inflammation in Autoimmune Disease. *J Immunol Res*, doi: 10.1155/2019/7403796.

93 Sun, Y., Qu, Y., Zhu, J. (2021). The Relationship Between Inflammation and Post-traumatic Stress Disorder. *Front Psychiatry*; 12. doi: 10.3389/fpsyt.2021.707543. PMID: 34456764; PMCID: PMC8385235.

94 Carlson, E.B., Palmieri, P.A., Field, N.P., Dalenberg, C.J., Macia, K.S., Spain, D.A. (2016). Contributions of Risk and Protective Factors to Prediction of Psychological Symptoms after Traumatic Experiences. *Comprehensive Psychiatry*, 69, 106–115. doi:10.1016/j.comppsych.2016.04.022

95 Crouch, E., Radcliff, E., Strompolis, M., Srivastav, A. (2018). Safe, Stable, and Nurtured: Protective Factors Against Poor Physical and Mental Health Outcomes Following Exposure to Adverse Childhood Experiences (Aces). *Journal of Child & Adolescent Trauma*, 12(2), 165–173. doi:10.1007/s40653-018-0217-9

96 Carlson, E.B., Palmieri, P.A., Field, N.P., Dalenberg, C.J., Macia, K.S., & Spain, D.A. (2016). Contributions of Risk and Protective Factors to Prediction of Psychological Symptoms after Traumatic Experiences. *Comprehensive Psychiatry*, 69, 106–115. doi:10.1016/j.comppsych.2016.04.022

97 American Psychiatric Association. (2022). *Diagnostic and Statistical Manual of Mental Disorders: DSM-5-TR*. American Psychiatric Association Publishing.

98 Boyer, S.M., Caplan, J.E., Edwards, L.K. (2022). Trauma-related Dissociation and the Dissociative Disorders. *Delaware Journal of Public Health*, 8(2), 78–84. https://doi.org/10.32481/djph.2022.05.010

99 Ibid.

100 Mitra, P., Jain, A. (2023). *Dissociative Identity Disorder*. StatPearls Publishing.

101 Gillig P.M. (2009). Dissociative Identity Disorder: A Controversial Diagnosis. *Psychiatry*, 6(3), 24–29.

102 Sloan, D.M., Wisco, B.E. (2014). Disclosure of Traumatic Events. In L.A. Zoellner, N.C. Feeny (eds.), *Facilitating Resilience and Recovery following Trauma* (pp. 191–209). The Guilford Press.

103 Ibid.

104 Lanius, R.A., Terpou, B.A., McKinnon, M.C. (2020). The Sense of Self in the Aftermath of Trauma: Lessons from the Default Mode Network in Posttraumatic Stress Disorder. *European Journal of Psychotraumatology*, 11(1). https://doi.org/10.1080/20008198.2020.1807703

105 Thompson, B., Koenig Kellas, J., Soliz, J., Thompson, J., Epp, A., Schrodt, P. (2009). Family Legacies. *Narrative Inquiry*, 19(1), 106–134. https://doi.org/10.1075/ni.19.1.07tho

106 Ibid.

107 Rohrer, J.M., Egloff, B., & Schmukle, S.C. (2015). Examining the Effects of Birth Order on Personality. *Proceedings of the National Academy of Sciences*, 112(46), 14224–14229. https://doi.org/10.1073/pnas.1506451112

108 Horner, P., Andrade, F., Delva, J., Grogan-Kaylor, A., Castillo, M. (2012). The Relationship of Birth Order and Gender with Academic Standing and Substance Use among Youth in Latin America. *Journal of Individual Psychology*, 68(1), 19–37.

109 Wu, K., Kim, J.H.J., Nagata, D.K., Kim, S.I. (2018). Perceptions of Sibling Relationships and Birth Order among Asian American and European American Emerging Adults. *Journal of Family Issues*, 39(13), 3641–3663. https://doi.org/10.1177/0192513X18783465
110 Ibid.
111 Rohrer, J.M., Egloff, B., Schmukle, S.C. (2015). Examining the Effects of Birth Order on Personality. *Proceedings of the National Academy of Sciences of the United States of America*, 112(46), 14224–14229. https://doi.org/10.1073/pnas.1506451112
112 Adler, A. (1964). *Problems of Neurosis*. Harper Torchbooks.
113 Fukuya, Y., Fujiwara, T., Isumi, A., Doi, S., Ochi, M. (2021). Association of Birth Order with Mental Health Problems, Self-Esteem, Resilience, and Happiness among Children: Results from A-CHILD Study. *Frontiers in Psychiatry*, 12, 638088. https://doi.org/10.3389/fpsyt.2021.638088
114 Wu, K., Kim, J.H.J., Nagata, D.K., Kim, S.I. (2018). Perceptions of Sibling Relationships and Birth Order among Asian American and European American Emerging Adults. *Journal of Family Issues*, 39(13), 3641–3663. https://doi.org/10.1177/0192513X18783465
115 Wolicki, S.B., Bitsko, R.H., Cree, R.A., Danielson, M.L., Ko, J.Y., Warner, L., Robinson, L.R. (2021). Mental Health of Parents and Primary Caregivers by Sex and Associated Child Health Indicators. *Adv Res Sci*, 2, 125–139. https://doi.org/10.1007/s42844-021-00037-7
116 Fekadu, W., Mihiretu, A., Craig, T.K.J., Fekadu, A. (2019). Multidimensional Impact of Severe Mental Illness on Family Members: Systematic Review. *BMJ Open*, 9(12), e032391. https://doi.org/10.1136/bmjopen-2019-032391
117 Ennis, E., Bunting, B.P. (2013). Family Burden, Family Health and Personal Mental Health. *BMC Public Health*, 13(1). https://doi.org/10.1186/1471-2458-13-255

118 Ibid.; Sullivan, A.B., Miller, D. (2015). Who Is Taking Care of the Caregiver? *Journal of Patient Experience*, 2(1), 7–12. doi:10.1177/237437431500200103

119 Cham, C.Q., Ibrahim, N., Siau, C.S., Kalaman, C.R., Ho, M.C., Yahya, A.N., Visvalingam, U. et al. (2022). Caregiver Burden among Caregivers of Patients with Mental Illness: A Systematic Review and Meta-Analysis. *Healthcare (Basel)*, 10(12), 2423. doi: 10.3390/healthcare10122423. PMID: 36553947; PMCID: PMC9777672.

120 Burnley, C.S. (1987). Caregiving: The Impact on Emotional Support for Single Women. *Journal of Aging Studies*, 1(3), 253–264. https://doi.org/10.1016/0890-4065(87)90017-X

121 Leijdesdorff, S., van Doesum, K., Popma, A., Klaassen, R., van Amelsvoort, T. (2017). Prevalence of Psychopathology in Children of Parents with Mental Illness and/or Addiction: An Up to Date Narrative Review. *Curr Opin Psychiatry*, 30(4), 312–317. doi: 10.1097/YCO.0000000000000341. PMID: 28441171.

122 Martinez, B., Pechlivanoglou, P., Meng, D., Traubici, B., Mahood, Q., Korczak, D., Colasanto, M. et al. (2022). Clinical Health Outcomes of Siblings of Children with Chronic Conditions: A Systematic Review and Meta-Analysis. *The Journal of Pediatrics*, 250. https://doi.org/10.1016/j.jpeds.2022.07.002

123 Kessler, R.C., Berglund, P., Demler, O., Jin, R., Merikangas, K.R., Walters, E.E. (2005). Lifetime Prevalence and Age-of-Onset Distributions of DSM-IV Disorders in the National Comorbidity Survey Replication. *Archives of General Psychiatry*, 62(6), 593–602. doi:10.1001/archpsyc.62.6.593; Spencer, L., McGovern, R., Kaner, E., (2022). A Qualitative Exploration of 14 to 17-Year Old Adolescents' Views of Early and Preventative Mental Health Support in Schools. *Journal of*

Public Health, 44(2), 363–369, https://doi.org/10.1093/pubmed/fdaa214
124 Collins, N.L. (1996). Revised Adult Attachment Scale (RAAS) [Database record]. APA PsycTests. https://doi.org/10.1037/t19162-000
125 Chopik, W.J., Kitayama, S. (2018). Personality Change Across the Life Span: Insights from a Cross-Cultural, Longitudinal Study. *Journal of Personality*, 86(3), 508–521. https://doi.org/10.1111/jopy.12332
126 Ibid.
127 Wu, K., Kim, J.H.J., Nagata, D.K., Kim, S.I. (2018). Perceptions of Sibling Relationships and Birth Order among Asian American and European American Emerging Adults. *Journal of Family Issues*, 39(13), 3641–3663. https://doi.org/10.1177/0192513X18783465
128 Ibid.
129 Soulsby, L.K., Bennett, K.M. (2015). Marriage and Psychological Wellbeing: The Role of Social Support. *Psychology*, 6(11), 1349–1359. https://doi.org/10.4236/psych.2015.611132
130 Rosenfeld, E. The Fire that Changed the Way We Think About Grief. (2018). Harvard Crimson. https://www.thecrimson.com/article/2018/11/29/erich-lindemann-cocoanut-grove-fire-grief/.
131 Grief. (n.d.). American Psychological Association. https://www.apa.org/topics/grief
132 Grief, Bereavement, and Coping with Loss (PDQ®). (n.d.). National Cancer Institute. https://www.cancer.gov/about-cancer/advanced-cancer/caregivers/planning/bereavement-hp-pdq
133 Zisook, S., Shear, K. (2009). Grief and Bereavement: What Psychiatrists Need to Know. *World Psychiatry*, 8(2), 67–74. https://doi.org/10.1002/j.2051-5545.2009.tb00217.

134 Miller, M.D. Complicated Grief in Late Life. (2012). *Dialogues Clin Neurosci*, 14(2):195–202. doi: 10.31887/DCNS.2012.14.2/mmiller. PMID: 22754292; PMCID: PMC3384448.
135 Zisook, S., Shear, K. (2009). Grief and Bereavement: What Psychiatrists Need to Know. *World Psychiatry*, 8(2), 67–74. https://doi.org/10.1002/j.2051-5545.2009.tb00217.
136 O'Connor, M.F. (2019). Grief: A Brief History of Research on How Body, Mind, and Brain Adapt. *Psychosom Med*, 81(8), 731–738. doi: 10.1097/PSY.0000000000000717
137 Ibid.
138 Defense Mechanism. APA Dictionary of Psychology. (n.d.). American Psychological Association. https://dictionary.apa.org/defense-mechanism
139 Feldman, S.S., Araujo, K.B., Steiner, H. (1996). Defense Mechanisms in Adolescents as a Function of Age, Sex, and Mental Health Status. *Journal of the American Academy of Child and Adolescent Psychiatry*, 35(10), 1344–1354. https://doi.org/10.1097/00004583-199610000-00022
140 Swaminath G. (2006). 'Joke's a Part': In Defence of Humour. *Indian J Psychiatry*, 48(3), 177–80. doi: 10.4103/0019-5545.31581. PMID: 20844648; PMCID: PMC2932988.
141 Dozois, D.J.A., Beck, A.T. (2008). Cognitive Schemas, Beliefs, and Assumptions. In K.S. Dobson D.J.A. Dozois (eds.), *Risk Factors in Depression* (pp. 121–143). Elsevier Academic Press. https://doi.org/10.1016/B978-0-08-045078-0.00006-X; Chand, S.P., Kuckel, D.P., Huecker, M.R. (2023). *Cognitive Behavior Therapy*. StatPearls Publishing.
142 Ibid.

www.ingramcontent.com/pod-product-compliance
Lightning Source LLC
Chambersburg PA
CBHW020540030426
42337CB00013B/918